Wild Morsels

Written and illustrated
by Angela Stafford

© Angela Stafford 2005
http://www.wildmorsels.com
info@wildmorsels.com
ISBN: 0-646-44561-8

All rights reserved. No part of this publication may be reproduced, stored in a retrieval system, or transmitted in any form or by any means, electronic, mechanical, photocopying, recording or otherwise without the prior permission in writing of the author.

Acknowledgements

Mitchell Stafford — my husband: Thank you for coming up with the idea for this book, for your continual encouragement, your keen editor's eye and for being my number one recipe tester!

Bob Foster — my Uncle: Thank you for testing my recipes and introducing me to the wonderful world of cooking.

Lynne Blackman — my mum: Thank you for testing my recipes, inspiring and encouraging me.

Shanta — my Aunty: Thank you for testing my recipes and all your encouragement.

Denise Thorpe — my Aunty: Thank you for your time spent editing.

Natalie Grainger — friend: Fellow foodie — Thank you for your time spent editing and testing recipes.

Kel Blackman — my Dad: Thank you for your time spent editing, teaching me and testing my recipes.

Nikki Blackman — my sister: Thank you for testing my recipes and talking food and recipe ideas.

Pam Roberts — friend: Thank you for testing my recipes and giving feedback.

Ethan Stafford — my Son: Thank you for learning to sleep so I could get this book finished.

Debbie Bainbridge — friend: Fellow foodie — Thank you for testing my recipes and for our endless foodie discussions and ideas.

About the Author

One night in October 1974, at a Sydney hospital, the excited crowd was gathering around a highly screened baby display window into the newborns' nursery. They were all ready to get a glimpse of *their* special baby. I was there, in my new role of uncle, to sight my new niece, Angela.

At precisely 8 o'clock the heavy curtain started to open, showing the unsuspecting occupants of the nursery. The crowd now surged forward in a frenzy, voices rising several octaves and decibels, as they eagerly searched through the shrivelled-faced screaming rows for *their* baby. Me too...and there she was...Angela, with a wooden spoon in her tiny hand.

As Angela grew she developed a strong interest in the production and consumption of food. Like me, this fascination increased and was incorporated into her identity in her early 20s. Whilst I continued producing dishes on a Wagnerian scale (with at least 10 freshly ground spices) and desserts of flavoured, congealed cholesterol, Angela was defecting to the health food camp. Tasty and ridiculously healthy treats emerged from her imagination and kitchen.

Like other relatives, I was asked to 'test' many of these recipes for this book...more of a sneaky way of recruiting converts! I must confess many of these recipes are now part of my cooking repertoire.

So as the curtain opens on this book of tasty vegan treats, and the feeding frenzy begins, there are more and more converts, to tasty, healthy recipes, surging towards the dinner table...including Angela's son, whose first words included *tofu* and *lentils*.

Let's eat!

Angela's Uncle Bob.

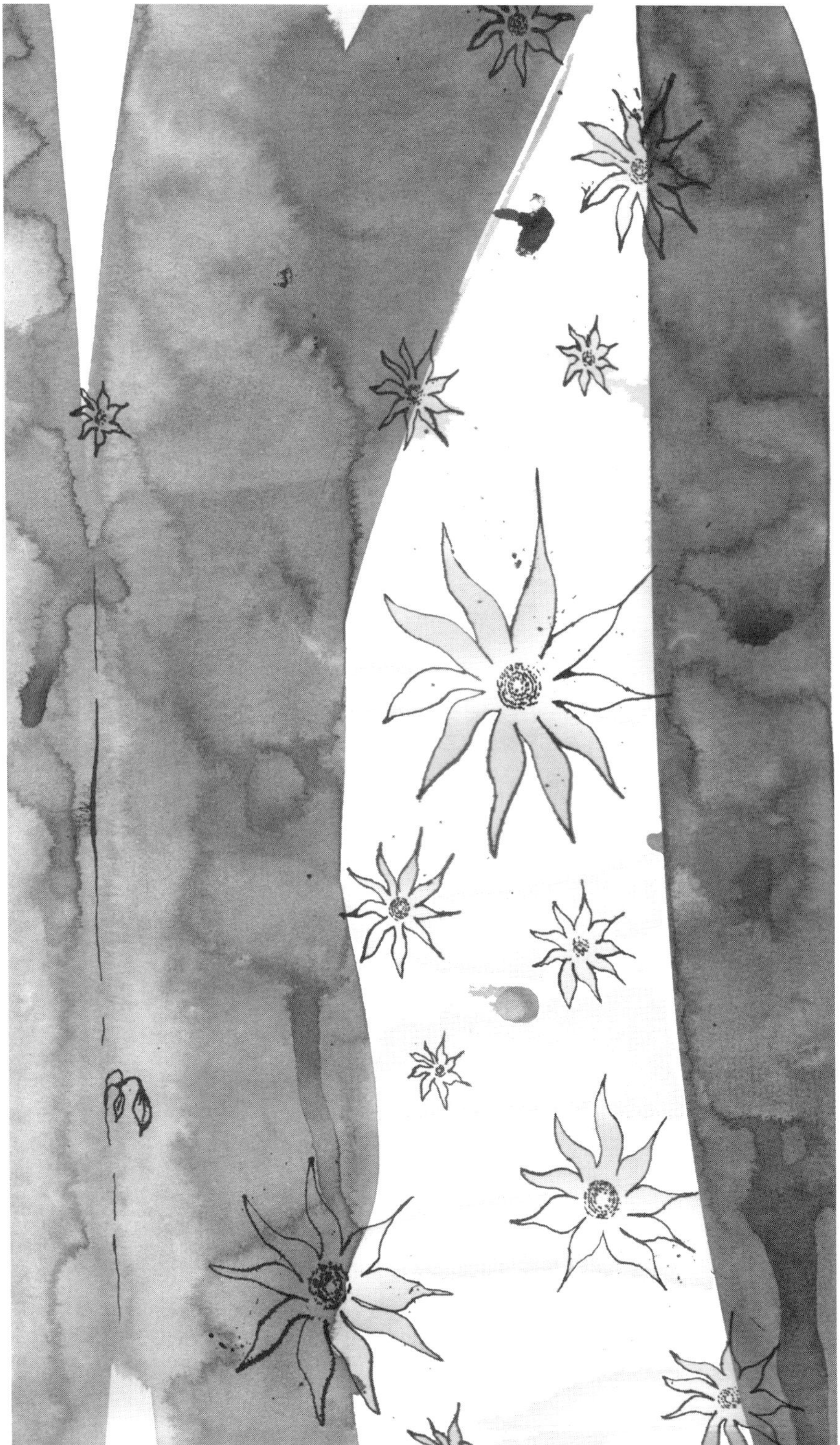

Contents

Welcome to the Wild Kitchen   3
Defining Differences   4

Cooking Tips and Pointers   6
Creative cooking   6
Conversion Tables   7
Name Variations   8
Alternative ingredients   9
Cooking dried beans and lentils   14
Cooking great rice   22
Cooking Couscous   23
Making your own breadcrumbs   24
Bleeding eggplants   25
A note on vitamin B12   25

Breakfast   27
Sweet Fruity Muesli   28
Toasted Muesli   29
Almond Spice Crunch   30
Apple & Spice Porridge   31
American-Style Breakfast Potatoes   32
Tofu Scramble   33
Buckwheat & Molasses Pikelets   34
Pancakes   35
Luxurious Fruit Salad   36
Breakfast Smoothie   37
Fruit Slush   37

Snacks, Sides & Starters   39

Riviera Burgers   40
Summer Rice Burgers   41
Mexican Patties   42
Spicy Potato Patties   43
Moorish Lentil Balls   44
Mexican Bites   45
Japanese Rice Balls   46
Crumbed Tofu Schnitzels   47
Not-Sausage Rolls   48
Tortilla Sandwiches   49
Vegetable Curry Parcels   50
Savoury Scrolls   52
Spring Rolls   54
Oven Chips   55
Karelien Potato Pies   56
Mixed Vegetable Bake   58
Carrots & Beans in Tomato Zest   59
Rosemary & Lime Potatoes   59
Pumpkin & Sweet Potato Fusion   60
Hazelnutty Beans   61
Mekong Asparagus   61

Salads   63

Tomato Salsa Salad   64
Italian Salad   64
Wild Rice Salad   65
Refreshing Bean Boost   66
Mitchell's Red Salad   67
Sesame Salad   67
Mango & Avocado Salad   68
Mostly Green Salad   69
Roasted Vegetable & Couscous Salad   70
Mixed Seed Salad   71
Tomato & Basil Salad   71

Soups   73
Carrot and Coriander Soup   74
Middle Eastern Vegetable Soup   75
Tomato and Basil Soup   76
Shanta's Pumpkin Soup   77
Thai Vegetable Soup   78
Tomato and Lentil Soup   79
Wild Winter Warm-up   80
Creamy Vegetable Soup   81
Potato, Pea and Mint Soup   82
Corn Chowder   83
Minestrone Soup   84
Turkish Bean Soup   85

Main Dishes - Tofu & Vegetables   87
Shanta's Nifty Tofu Tip   88
Saucy Garlic Potatoes with Dill   89
Moroccan Vegetables with Couscous   90
Dilled Spinach with Mushrooms   91
Mixed Vegetable & Apricot Curry   92
Pumpkin & Sweet Potato Masala   93
Vegetables and Tofu in Sweet Tamari Marinade   94
Mushroom Steaks   95
Lemon & Thyme Roast   96
Bombay Potatoes   97
Vegetable and Tofu Stroganoff   98
Eggplant Wraps with Minted Couscous   100

Main Dishes - Beans and Pulses   103
Indian Dahl   104
Two Lentil Dahl   105
Chilli Con Carne   106
Gentle Lentil Stew   107
Vegetable Dhansak   108
Golden Masala   110
Bean and Spinach Stew   111
Lentil and Bean Stew   112
Potato and Lentil Bake   113

Moroccan Chickpea Casserole   114
Lentil Loaf   115
Lentil and Barley Shepherd's Pie   116
Burritos   118
Boston Barbecue Beans   120
Aduki Bean Stir Fry   121

Main Dishes - Rice and Pasta   123

Spaghetti Bolognese   124
Henna's Sunflower and Bean Pasta   125
Pesto & Tomato Spaghetti   126
Herb Pasta with Sun-dried Tomatoes & Spinach   127
Vegetable Lasagne   128
Roasted Capsicum Pasta   130
Satay Vegetables & Soba Noodles   131
Pad Thai   132
Cashew Soba Noodles   134
Roasted Pumpkin Fried Rice   135
Wild Fried Rice   136
Vegetable Pilau   137
Mediterranean Vegetable Risotto   138

Sauces & Dips   141

Cashew & Pepper Gravy   142
Peanut Sauce   143
Fresh Tomato Sauce   144
Barbecue Sauce   145
Pizza Sauce   146
Asian Dipping Sauce   147
Mint Dipping Sauce   147
Tomato Salsa   148
Baba Ganoush   148
Homous   149
Refreshing Guacamole   150
Roasted Capsicum & Cashew Pesto   151

Baked Goodies   153
Vegan Baking Tips   154
Chocolate Coconut Biscuits   155
Cinnamon Biscuits   156
Oat & Malt Biscuits   157
Peanut Butter Biscuits   158
Passion Stars   159
American Style Choc Chip Cookies   160
Lemon Coconut Biscuits   161
Chocolate Brownies   162
Banana & Walnut Muffins   163
Apple & Cinnamon Muffins   164
Berry Chocolate Muffins   165
Date Loaf   166
Blueberry Cake   167
Chocolate Cake   168
Banana Cake   169

Desserts   171
Shortcrust Pastry   172
Shortcrust Flan Pastry   173
Apple Pie   174
Pumpkin Pie   175
Fruit Flan   176
Chocolate Tart   177
Baked Bananas with Maple and Pecan Cream   178
Citrus Mint Burst   179
Banana and Coconut Rice Pudding   180
Cashew Whipped Cream   181

Finale   182
Glossary of Ingredients   182
Suggested Reading List   189
Bibliography   190
Australian and New Zealand Societies   191
Index   193

"You put a baby in a crib with an apple and a rabbit. If it eats the rabbit and plays with the apple, I'll buy you a new car."
Harvey Diamond

Introduction

Welcome to the Wild Kitchen

> The purpose of this book is to open up the possibilities of cooking without animal products. It is easy to cook a huge variety of natural food that is delicious and very healthy – not only for the body, but also for the environment and the conscience.

The recipes that follow contain no animal products at all – animal products including meat, dairy, eggs and honey. For this reason, it is a pure vegan cookbook and all recipes suit both vegan and vegetarian diets. However you don't need to take a completely vegan approach if it does not suit you at this point. For example, the recipes will work just as well with dairy products. Rice and soy milks, cheeses and yoghurt may be replaced with their dairy equivalents. The aim of this book is not to target a select group of people but rather to help everyone take a step towards a healthier lifestyle by starting in the kitchen. It may also serve as a creative guide to developing meals that suit your personal tastes and preferences. By using the creative ideas included with many of the recipes, you are sure to develop confidence during the cooking process.

Defining Differences

Not everyone is familiar with the nature of a vegan or vegetarian lifestyle. There is a lot of confusion about what foods are included in these diets and as a result, having a vegan or vegetarian to dinner can, for some people, be an anxious experience. There is a lot of vegetarian information available and I have included a suggested reading list at the back of this book for those who wish to learn more. For the moment however, let me just say that by taking a step in this direction you will gain not only huge health benefits, but you will also be addressing environmental and humanitarian concerns that face us today. Issues such as the effect the meat and dairy industries have on the environment, and what the animals raised for food go through during their short, often horrific lives. The destructive effect of not only meat, but also other animal products, on the body and the environment.

Vegetarians

A vegetarian does not eat any part of an animal. This includes red and white flesh, so chicken and fish are both off the menu. However vegetarians do eat dairy and honey, as although they are animal products, the animal is not killed to obtain them. This is not to say all vegetarians choose this diet for humanitarian reasons, some do it for health benefits or because they do not like the taste of meat, but the bottom line is the same, and that is that there is no consumption of animal flesh.

No, I am not suitable for vegetarians

"The word 'vegetarian' has only a passing connection with vegetables - it actually derives from the Latin word 'vegetus' meaning 'lively'"!
Australian Vegetarian Society Website

Vegans

A true vegan lifestyle is one that does not include the use or consumption of any animal products. On a dietary level, meat, dairy, eggs, honey, gelatine and some processed sugars are excluded from the diet as they all contain, or are animal products. A vegan lifestyle also excludes the use of leather, and animal skins.

Setting up a vegan lifestyle is getting easier. As the world becomes more aware of both vegan and vegetarian concerns, more products are becoming available. Replacing meat is not difficult as there are a huge variety of beans, seeds, nuts and pulses, all of which provide high levels of protein and nutrients. For those who still like the taste of meat, there are in many places meat substitutes, which are made of soy and vegetable proteins.

It is becoming easier to replace other non-vegan ingredients too. The section on alternative ingredients starting on page 9 includes milk, eggs, honey, sugar and meat.

Even replacing leather and furs is easy now. Most fashion stores stock clothes that look and feel like fur, but are actually made of synthetic materials. Leather is not the only material being used to make shoes, belts and wallets either. Contact your closest vegan society to find out the exact locations of animal friendly retailers.

Adjusting to a vegan or vegetarian lifestyle can range from difficult to very easy, depending on the individual and the environment, but I hope that this book provides some helpful suggestions on how to make the change. If you have no wish to change, then I hope this book at least provides you with an occasional alternative to the animal-based meal and/or prepares you for when you have a vegan or vegetarian guest.

Cooking Tips and Pointers

Creative cooking

Cooking does not have to be a chore, and let's face it, if you have chosen to adopt a vegan or vegetarian lifestyle, chances are, you are going to be spending some time in the kitchen making yourself wholesome meals that don't contain animal products. With this in mind, I suggest that you take a creative approach to cooking. The recipes in this book are the result of countless trials (and errors), experimentation, inspiration and hard work, and I found that the more I experimented and sought out new and tasty ingredients, the more fun cooking became.

Once you get the hang of vegan cooking, try branching out. Put on your favourite music and some comfortable clothes, make sure you start in a clean kitchen, use fresh produce whenever possible and let inspiration take over. Try modifying the ingredients a little, adding new flavours, looking at international cuisines and seeing if you can adapt some of the non-vegan dishes to healthy vegan alternatives.

Use the list of alternative ingredients starting on page 9 as a guide to adapting recipes or take a look in the glossary and learn about some new ingredients.

Whatever you put into the cooking process, you will get out of it. Often with very little effort and lots of fun, you can turn out healthy, tasty meals that will go towards saving our planet!

Conversion Tables

Unit	Metric	Imperial
1 teaspoon (tsp.)	5ml	1 tsp.
1 tablespoon (tblsp.)	15ml	1/2 fluid oz
3 teaspoons	1 tbsp.	1 tbsp.
1 cup	240ml	8 fluid oz
grams (g)	1g	.035 oz
	225g	8 oz
	500g	1.1 pounds
	1kg	2.2 pounds

Celcius	Fahrenheit
0°	32°
100°	212°
150°	300°
175°	350°
180°	356°
200°	400°
220°	425°

Introduction

Name Variations

There are a number of foods whose names vary between Australia, the United Kingdom and the United States. I have provided a list of the ones relevant to this book.

Australia	UK	USA
coriander	coriander	cilantro
capsicum	pepper	bell pepper
zucchini	courgette	zucchini
eggplant	aubergine	eggplant
pumpkin	butternut squash*	butternut squash*
chickpeas	chickpeas	garbanzo beans
biscuits	cookies/biscuits	cookies
beetroot	beetroot	beet
corn flour	corn flour	cornstarch
polenta	polenta	cornmeal
muesli	muesli	granola
wholemeal	wholemeal	whole wheat

* Apart from the Halloween period, fresh pumpkin is not widely available in the UK and USA. Butternut squash is very similar however, and the closest alternative.

Alternative ingredients

Following is a list of ingredients that are animal based and which are also widely used in the preparation of food. Below each heading is an explanation of the purpose they serve in recipes and the available alternatives for vegan cooking.

Meat

The majority of people are brought up on meat. It is usually considered the main source of iron and protein in a meal, and forms the staple for many recipes. For this reason, many people depend on its use to create what is considered to be a healthy and/or delicious meal. However, beans, lentils, nuts, grains and seeds can provide plenty of protein within a vegan diet. Iron is obtained through any of the following: sea vegetables, fortified bran flakes, oats, soybeans, chickpeas, blackstrap molasses, lentils, pumpkin seeds, tempeh, tofu, black beans, soy milk, dried apricots, kidney beans, beet greens, wheat germ, sunflower seeds, cashews, raisins.

Honey

The purpose of honey is as a sweetener, and also, obviously as a spread for breads and crackers. The primary honey replacement is rice syrup. It does not taste the same as honey, but has a sweet, natural flavour and has the same consistency as honey. It can be used as a replacement in recipes, and as a spread.

Milk

Milk has so many uses in cooking and is also considered a rich source of calcium. However, there are alternatives to animal milks, including soy milk, rice milk, oat milk and various milks of mixed grains and nuts, which usually come with a choice of flavoured, plain and calcium-enriched.

When cooking with alternative milks, substitution requires some discretion according to the taste the milk will add to your recipe, e.g. some milks are particularly nutty or grainy in flavour. I find the best overall substitutes to be soy milk and rice milk, but try out a few for yourself to see which suits you.

A major concern with a non-dairy diet is the maintenance of the body's calcium levels. The following foods will provide you with high levels of calcium: sesame seeds, leafy greens, almonds, beans, molasses, figs and tofu.

Yoghurt

Soy yoghurt is now widely available in supermarkets in both plain and flavoured. It does not taste exactly like dairy yoghurt but it does behave the same way in cooking. I have used it in a number of recipes to replace dairy yoghurt and dairy cream.

Cheese

The use of cheese in cooking is usually to provide flavour, but it is also used as a binder in many foods. The most typical example of this would be on the top of a pizza, where cheese holds the toppings together. Cheese is probably the toughest ingredient to replace. Nutritional value is not a problem because the calcium that cheese would usually provide is easily replaced with other healthy sources as previously listed. However, it is the consistency of cheese that is not always replicated in alternative ingredients. There are a number of alternative cheeses on the market, usually made with either soy or rice. They may not be readily available in all areas. When they are, although they may taste similar, they usually do not melt as well as dairy cheese or provide the same consistency. It comes down to the individual. You may choose to use the alternatives or to simply omit cheeses from your recipes and find alternative tastes. I have chosen, in this recipe book, to use alternative cheeses in only a few of the recipes.

Cow Liberaton Organisation

"Leave our tits alone!"

Eggs

The purpose of eggs in cooking is to bind the ingredients together. At first it may seem impossible to cook things like cakes and burgers without eggs, but on the contrary, there are many alternative binders. Below is a list of alternatives as well as the purpose for which they are best used. Throughout this book I have used tofu as my main binder but also included some recipes with soy flour and banana.

Egg replacer

There are a number of commercially-produced egg replacers on the market, most of which are made from potato starch and tapioca flour. The directions on the box will give a guide as to how much of the product will replace one egg. However, in this book, I have not used any commercial egg replacers in my recipes, not because they don't work, but because I prefer to use ingredients that I know will be available to everyone.

Mashed banana

A particularly good binder in cakes and puddings. Of course, there will also be the strong banana flavour. The amount of banana needed will depend on the recipe but I find that generally 1 banana = 1 egg.

Silken tofu

Tofu is a particularly good binder in cakes, brownies and puddings.
5 tbsp. pureed tofu = 1 egg

Soy flour

Add to the liquid in your recipe.
1 tbsp. = 1 egg

The egg is no longer indispensable

Sugars

During the refining of sugar, the charred bones of animals are used, making it a non-vegan product. However, any sugar that is unrefined will be vegan and you would be surprised how many varieties of sugar are unrefined. Look out for brown, muscavado and Demerara sugars, as often there are many brands that state that their products are unrefined. Below is a general list of alternative sweeteners. For further information on the particular products and where to get them, please see the glossary.

Liquid Sweeteners

Include rice syrup, maple syrup, barley malt, black strap molasses, agave syrup and fruit juices, each giving their own unique flavour.

Crystal Sweeteners

Include date sugar, fructose, sucanat, Demerara, muscavado and many brown sugars. Just check the packaging for the word "unrefined" and this will indicate a vegan product. I have tried to vary the sweetening methods in my recipes so as not to be limited to one or two products. I have also chosen not to use products such as date sugar or sucanat specifically, in case they are not available to everyone. Therefore, when using a crystal sweetener, I have simply specified the use of an unrefined sugar.

Gelatine

Gelatine is produced from animal bones and is therefore not vegan or vegetarian. However, a product named agar agar, made from a sea vegetable, will do the same job. It is available in health food shops and Asian supermarkets.

> "If the divine creator has taken pain to give us delicious and exquisite things to eat, the least we can do is prepare them well and serve them with ceremony"
> Fernand Point (1897-1955)

Cooking dried beans and lentils

I think that if you have the time, cooking your own dried beans and lentils is preferable to using tinned ones. Tinned beans contain preservatives, and often, added salt and sugar. They are sometimes a little mushy and don't absorb as much flavour from the dish you are adding them to if they are already completely cooked. Of course, there will always be times when you just don't have the time and tinned beans are your only option. Just remember when buying your beans to check the ingredients list for hidden additives. It is possible to buy them without sugar and salt added, and you will find that organic beans taste a lot better.

When cooking your own beans, it is often a good idea to cook more than you need as they may be frozen and used later, saving you the trouble of cooking or using tinned beans at a moment's notice. The general rule is 1 cup of dried equals 2½-3 cups of cooked.

In the pages ahead are guidelines for soaking and cooking different beans. I have provided directions for soaked beans because soaking them will not only reduce cooking time, but will also remove a lot of the indigestible element of the bean, associated with flatulence. Another way of reducing the flatulent effect of beans is to add spinach, kale, or a seaweed such as Kombu, to the recipe.

If you want to cook the beans without soaking, simply lengthen the cooking time and never add any seasoning until the bean has already started to become tender, otherwise the salt may prevent the bean from softening.

In all of my recipes, I have included both the dried and the cooked measurements for beans where applicable (some are not available in a tin). This way you have the option of cooking them from scratch or using the tinned kind.

General rules for cooking all beans and lentils.

- 1 cup dried equals approximately 2½–3 cups cooked. See specific beans (overleaf) for variations.
- Always use cold, soft water for cooking. The heavy metals in hard water, or any metals picked up by hot water in the pipes, will prevent the beans from softening.
- If your water is too hard, use purified water or add a pinch of baking soda to hard water.
- When cooking the beans, cover with about 2cm of cold water and top up later if necessary.
- Always refrigerate beans after cooking if you are not using them straight away, to prevent fermentation.
- Always discard any grey or brown coloured foam from the cooking beans, as this contains the indigestible element.
- To further reduce the risk of flatulence:

    ### Blanch your beans:
    1) Cover soaked beans in cold water and bring to the boil.
    2) Boil rapidly for 5 minutes.
    3) Remove from heat and rinse thoroughly.
    4) Continue cooking as directed.

Please note that all cooking times in this section are for blanched beans.

Pinto/Borlotti beans (1 cup dried = 3 cups cooked)

Soaking the beans
Pinto beans should be soaked for at least 6 hours in cold water. Change the water a couple of times. Once the beans are soaked, rinse them thoroughly and place in a saucepan with cold water.

Blanch the beans according to the directions on page 15. If you decide not to blanch the beans, the cooking time will be longer than specified below.

Cooking the beans
Bring beans to the boil, and boil rapidly for 10 minutes. Reduce heat to the lowest setting and simmer until the beans are soft (this should take 25 minutes). Throughout the cooking, top up water when it runs low and stir occasionally. If you wish to salt the beans, do not add it until at least halfway through cooking, when the beans are tender.

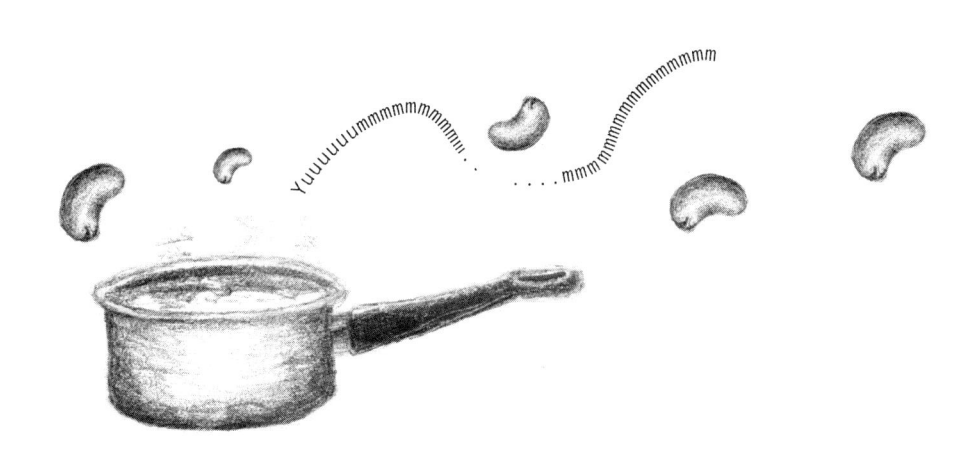

Blackeye beans/peas (1 cup dried = 2.5 cups cooked)

Blackeye beans, sometimes referred to as blackeye peas, do not require soaking.

Blanch the beans according to the directions on page 15. If you decide not to blanch the beans, the cooking time will be longer than specified below.

Cooking the beans
Bring beans to the boil, and boil rapidly for 10 minutes. Reduce heat to the lowest setting and simmer until the beans are soft (this should take 15 minutes). Throughout the cooking, top up water when it runs low and stir occasionally.

Red kidney beans (1 cup dried = 3 cups cooked)

Soaking the beans
Kidney beans should be soaked for at least 8 hours in cold water. Change the water a couple of times. Once the beans are soaked, rinse them thoroughly and place in a saucepan with cold water.

Blanch the beans according to the directions on page 15. If you decide not to blanch the beans, the cooking time will be longer than specified below.

Cooking the beans
Bring beans to the boil, and boil rapidly for 10 minutes. Reduce heat to the lowest setting and simmer until the beans are soft (this should take 20 minutes). Throughout the cooking, top up water when it runs low and stir occasionally. If you wish to salt the beans, do not add it until at least halfway through cooking, when the beans are tender.

Canellini/Navy beans (1 cup dried = 2.5 cups cooked)

Soaking the beans
Canellini beans should be soaked for at least 6 hours in cold water. Change the water a couple of times. Once the beans are soaked, rinse them thoroughly and place in a saucepan with cold water.

Blanch the beans according to the directions on page 15. If you decide not to blanch the beans, the cooking time will be longer than specified below.

Cooking the beans
Bring beans to the boil, and boil rapidly for 10 minutes. Reduce heat to the lowest setting and simmer until the beans are soft (this should take 15 minutes). Throughout the cooking, top up water when it runs low and stir occasionally. If you wish to salt the beans, do not add it until at least halfway through cooking, when the beans are tender.

Aduki Beans (1 cup dried = 3 cups cooked)

Soaking the beans
Aduki beans should be soaked for at least 8 hours in cold water. Change the water a couple of times. Once the beans are soaked, rinse them thoroughly and place in a saucepan with cold water.

Blanch the beans according to the directions on page 15. If you decide not to blanch the beans, the cooking time will be longer than specified below.

Cooking the beans
Bring beans to the boil, and boil rapidly for 10 minutes. Reduce heat to the lowest setting and simmer until the beans are soft (this should take 15 minutes). Throughout the cooking, top up water when it runs low and stir occasionally. If you wish to salt the beans, do not add it until at least halfway through cooking, when the beans are tender.

Chickpeas (1 cup dried = 2.5 cups cooked)

Soaking the beans
Chickpeas are one of the hardest of all legumes and should be soaked for 10 hours in cold water. Change the water a few times. Once the beans are soaked, rinse them thoroughly and place in a saucepan with cold water.

Blanch the beans according to the directions on page 15. If you decide not to blanch the beans, the cooking time will be longer than specified below.

Cooking the beans
Bring beans to the boil, and boil rapidly for 10 minutes. Reduce heat to the lowest setting and simmer until the beans are soft (this should take 50 minutes). Throughout the cooking, top up water when it runs low and stir occasionally. If you wish to salt the beans, do not add it until at least halfway through cooking, when the beans are tender.

Red lentils (1 cup dried = 3 cups cooked)

Soaking the lentils

Red lentils do not require any soaking, but always rinse them a number of times before cooking. Try to get the water around them as clear as possible to make them more digestible and to remove the grit that is often present.

You may wish to blanch the lentils but I prefer to just rinse them well — mainly because blanching them almost cooks them right through and they absorb a lot more flavour if they are added to a dish as they are. If you have a real problem with digesting red lentils, then you may wish to blanch them anyway (see page 15 for instructions). After doing this, you will need to reduce the water in the recipe you are using by about half. Add the water gradually to prevent over liquefying the dish.

Cooking the lentils (unblanched)

Use 2 cups of water to 1 cup of lentils and add a pinch of salt (this will help the lentils to cook at a steady rate and will add flavour). Place rinsed lentils into a saucepan with the water and salt. Bring to a rapid boil (this will take 4-5 minutes on a gas stove and a little longer on electric). Reduce the temperature to low and leave to simmer with the lid on for 20 minutes. After this time the lentils should be soft with a little water left. Make sure you scoop off any of the discoloured scum that rises to the top of the cooking water. Leave the lid on and remove pan from heat. Leave lentils to stand for a further 10 minutes so that all of the water can be absorbed.

Green/Brown lentils (1 cup dried = 3 cups cooked)

Soaking the lentils
Green lentils should be soaked for 4 hours in cold water. Change the water a couple of times. Once the lentils are soaked, rinse them thoroughly and place in a saucepan with cold water.

Blanch the lentils according to the directions on page 15. If you decide not to blanch the lentils, the cooking time will be longer than specified below.

Cooking the lentils
You will find that once the lentils are blanched, they will be cooked right the way through.

Green/Yellow split Peas (1 cup dried = 3 cups cooked)

Soaking the peas
Split peas can be soaked for 4 hours in cold water. Change the water a couple of times. Once the peas are soaked, rinse them thoroughly and place in a saucepan with cold water.

Blanch the peas according to the directions on page 15. If you decide not to blanch the peas, the cooking time will be longer than specified below.

Cooking the peas
You will find that once the peas are blanched, they will be almost cooked right the way through. All they need is another 5 minutes of rapid boiling and they are ready to eat.

The Passionate Pea Pot

Cooking great rice
(for those who don't have a rice cooker!)

White rice

Cooking good white rice is easy, once you know the formula. Use too much water, or over cook the rice and it can become gluggy and pasty, often ruining the meal. So, to create fluffy, tasty rice, follow the directions below. At first it may seem like more trouble than you are used to, but once you get a feel for it, and know what you are doing, it takes no effort.

1) Measure your rice so that you know how much water to use later. As a general rule, 1 cup of rice requires 1¼ cups of water.
2) Rinse your rice at least 4 times to remove the starch (this is the element that makes the rice sticky). Basically, the clearer the water becomes when you are rinsing it, the more starch you have removed.
3) Drain as much of the water as possible from your rinsed rice and place into a saucepan with the required amount of water.
4) Cover the saucepan and bring to the boil - watching to make sure it doesn't boil over.
5) Once the rice has boiled, reduce the heat to low and cook covered until the rice has absorbed most of the water. This should take about 8 minutes. DO NOT STIR THE RICE.
6) When you feel that most of the water has been absorbed, remove the saucepan from the heat and leave to stand with the lid on for 10 minutes. This will allow the rice to absorb any remaining water without burning to the bottom of the pan.
7) Fluff rice with a fork before serving.

Brown rice

Cooking good brown rice is usually just a matter of giving it plenty of time. Brown rice still contains the hard outer shell and so takes longer to cook. I try to use brown rice instead of white when possible because it still contains all the goodness that is lost during the refining of white rice.

1) Measure your rice so that you know how much water to use later. 1 cup of brown rice requires 1½ cups of water.
2) Brown rice only needs to be rinsed once. Drain as much of the water as possible from your rinsed rice and place into a saucepan with the required amount of water.
3) Cover the saucepan and bring to the boil – watching to make sure it doesn't boil over.
4) Once the rice has boiled, reduce the heat to low and cook covered until the rice has absorbed most of the water. This should take about 25 minutes. DO NOT STIR THE RICE.
5) When you feel that most of the water has been absorbed, remove the saucepan from the heat and leave to stand with the lid on for 10 minutes. This will allow the rice to absorb any remaining water without burning to the bottom of the pan.
6) Fluff rice with a fork before serving.

Cooking Couscous

1) Place measured amount of couscous into a small saucepan and measured amount of boiling water over the top. Exact measurements will be in the recipes but as a guide, 1 cup of couscous requires 1 cup of water.
2) Cover the saucepan for a few minutes until all water has been absorbed.
3) Put couscous over low heat and add vegan margarine (1 tbsp. per cup of couscous).
4) Fluff with a fork to separate the grains and serve.

Making your own breadcrumbs

Making your own breadcrumbs is a good idea, not only to use up bread that is no longer fresh, but also to ensure that you know exactly what is in your bread crumbs. Mass-produced packets of breadcrumbs can often be made from the lowest quality bread.

To make your breadcrumbs do one of the following:

1) Place slices or chunks of bread onto a baking tray. Bake in the oven at 180°C for 15-20 minutes until bread is very crispy.

OR

Place slices or chunks of bread onto a baking tray and leave in the hot sun until crispy.

2) Once your toasted bread is cool, blend in a food processor until the desired crumb is reached, (fine or coarse). Store in an airtight container, in a cool, dry place. Home-made breadcrumbs will last longer if stored in the fridge or freezer.

Bleeding eggplants

Eggplant will taste quite bitter unless you bleed it before it is cooked. To do this, cut the eggplant as required and then place into a bowl with plenty of salt. Toss the eggplant with the salt until it is well coated. Leave to stand for 10–15 minutes. You will notice that the eggplant will sweat a lot. This is the bitter tasting element of the vegetable. Rinse the eggplant well and cook as required.

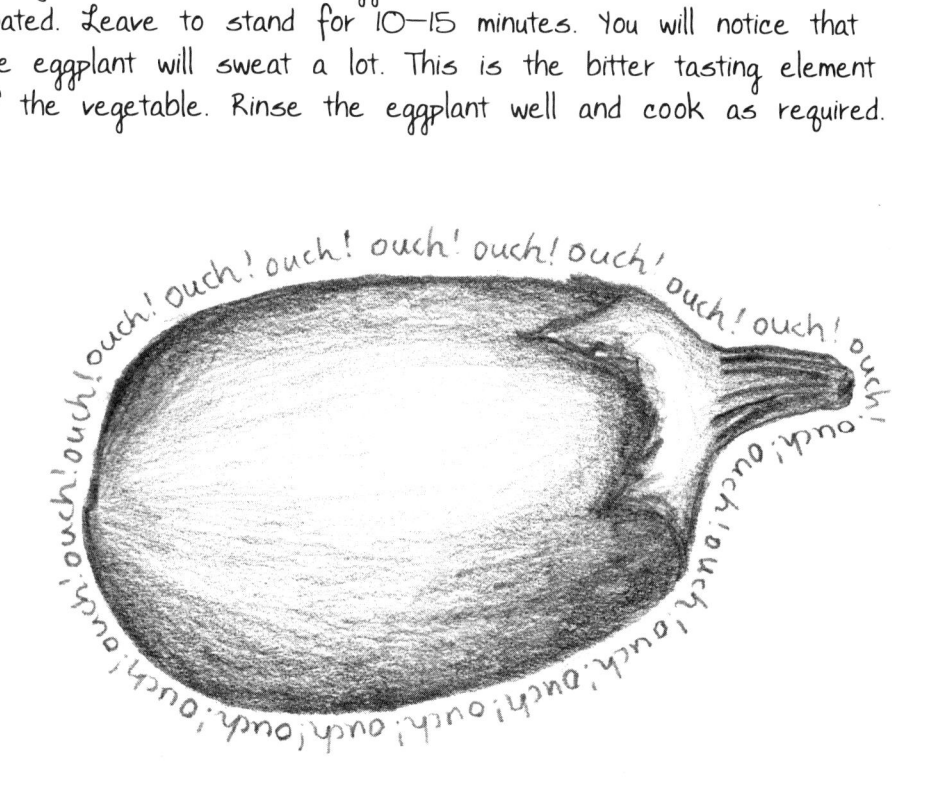

A note on vitamin B12

Vitamin B12 is an essential vitamin for the growth and development of children, the synthesis of red blood cells, and maintenance of the nervous system. This vitamin is primarily found in meat, dairy products and eggs but is also found in some plant foods and fortified products. However, if you decide to adopt a totally vegan diet, it is a good idea to take a vitamin B12 supplement to ensure that you are getting all of the nutrients you need. For more comprehensive information on the vitamin B12 issue and a list of fortified products, please contact your local vegan society. I have listed the various societies in the back of this book.

"Nothing will benefit human health and increase chances of survival for life on Earth as much as the evolution to a vegetarian diet".
Albert Einstein

Breakfast

Breakfast

Breakfast

Morning has broken

Sweet Fruity Muesli

Approximately 14 servings

I have this for breakfast every morning and I find it is a great start to the day, especially topped with a banana or other fresh fruit.

creative tip

This is just a basic mix and any number of ingredients can be added to this recipe. Some further suggestions are wheatgerm, lecithin, oatbran, soy flakes, puffed wheat, puffed millet, puffed corn, or other dried fruits and nuts.

5 cups rolled oats
2 cups unsweetened puffed rice
1 cup chopped dried apricots
1 cup chopped dried apple
1 cup currants or sultanas
1 cup sunflower seeds
1 cup sesame seeds*
1 cup slivered almonds
1 cup desiccated coconut

* It is best to split the sesame seeds in a mortar and pestle to release the calcium

1) Mix all ingredients together in a large bowl and store in an airtight container.
2) Serve with chilled rice or soy milk.

Toasted Muesli

Approximately 5 servings

If you prefer toasted muesli to the raw kind, this is a simple conversion of the Sweet Fruity Muesli on the previous page.

creative tip — You don't have to sweeten the muesli with molasses. You can use rice syrup, date syrup or barley malt.

1½ cups apple juice
1 tbsp. blackstrap molasses
5 cups of Sweet Fruity Muesli (page 28)

1) Pre-heat oven to 180°C.
2) In a small saucepan, mix apple juice and molasses over medium heat until the molasses melts into the juice.
3) In a large mixing bowl, combine the liquid and the muesli until all grains and oats are well coated.
4) Spread muesli over ungreased, nonstick baking trays so that there is a thin, even cover.
5) Place in the oven and cook for 10 minutes or until the muesli is brown and toasty.
6) Leave to cool and dry, and then seal in an airtight container.
7) Serve with chilled soy or rice milk.

Almond Spice Crunch

Approximately 10 servings

Another baked cereal, rich in flavour and quite different to the other muesli recipes.

creative tip — You could add different dried fruits and/or other nuts and flaked coconut.

2 cups rolled oats
2 tbsp. ground arrowroot
1 tsp. ground ginger
¼ tsp. ground cloves
1 tsp. ground cinnamon
½ tsp. ground nutmeg
½ cup rice syrup
2 tsp. vanilla extract
5 tbsp. sunflower oil
3 cups natural cornflakes
1 cup flaked almonds

1) Pre-heat oven to 180°C.
2) In a medium-sized mixing bowl, combine rolled oats, arrowroot, ginger, cloves, cinnamon and nutmeg.
3) Add the rice syrup, vanilla extract and oil, and stir until well combined.
4) Press mixture into an ungreased 32cm x 18cm shallow baking tray. It will be a very thin layer resulting in a crunchy biscuit once cooked.
5) Bake for 20 minutes, or until brown and crispy.
6) Turn onto a cooling rack and leave until it is completely cold.
7) Crumble the slab into small pieces and then combine with the cornflakes and almonds.
8) Serve with chilled soy or rice milk.

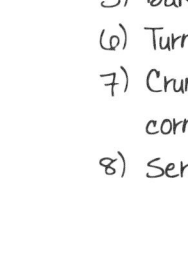

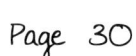

Apple & Spice Porridge

Serves 2

This is delicious on a cold morning.

2 ½ cups water
1 cup quick oats
1 apple, peeled and grated
½ tsp. ground cinnamon
½ tsp. ground nutmeg
soy or rice milk (optional)
Pure maple syrup (to sweeten)

Note: This recipe requires constant stirring so it is best to have all ingredients measured and ready before cooking.

1) Place all ingredients into a medium-sized saucepan and mix well.
2) Bring to the boil and then reduce to simmer. Stir for 2-3 minutes.
3) Serve in 2 bowls with a little soy/rice milk and maple syrup to sweeten (note that the apple has already provided some sweetness).

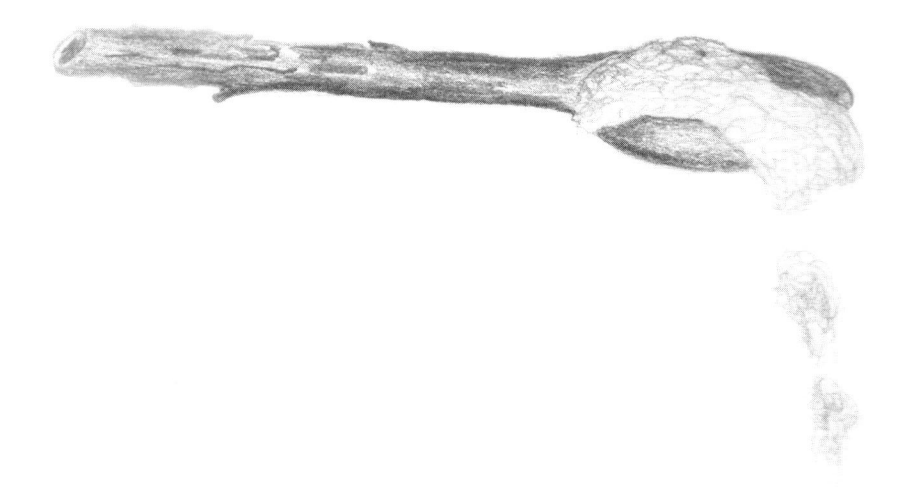

American-Style Breakfast Potatoes

Serves 2

Fried potatoes are a favourite item on the breakfast menu in the USA. However they can be enjoyed at any meal.

5 medium-sized potatoes, (approx. 750g)
2 spring onions, finely chopped
2 tbsp. olive oil
2 cloves garlic, crushed
1 tsp. ground paprika
1 tsp. dried parsley
1 tsp. dried thyme
1 tsp. dried oregano
½ tsp. sea salt
Freshly ground black pepper, to season

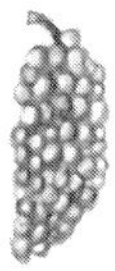

1) Scrub potatoes and cut into cubes.
2) Steam until just tender (this should take about 10 minutes but it will depend on the size of the pieces).
3) In a frying pan, stir fry the spring onions in the olive oil until soft.
4) Add the garlic, paprika and potatoes. Stir to coat.
5) Add remaining ingredients and keep tossing until potatoes are soft (10-15 minutes).
6) Serve hot.

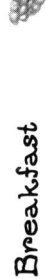

Tofu Scramble

Serves 2

For those who like a hot breakfast try this alternative to scrambled eggs.

350g silken tofu
¼ tsp. turmeric
¼ tsp. ground paprika
2 tsp. tamari sauce
1 spring onion, finely chopped
½ capsicum, diced
½ cup sliced mushrooms
1 tbsp. olive oil
Pinch of sea salt
Freshly ground black pepper, to season

1) Mash tofu with a fork and then mix in the turmeric, paprika and tamari sauce until evenly distributed. Set aside.
2) In a small frying pan, fry the spring onion, capsicum and mushrooms in the olive oil until tender.
3) Add the tofu mixture and mix well.
4) Season with salt and pepper and cook for 5-7 minutes, stirring often.
5) Serve on toast or with fried tomatoes.

Tofu scramble comes highly recommended by Reginald Peckerhead II of Old McDonald Farm.

Buckwheat & Molasses Pikelets

Makes 30 standard-size pikelets

These pikelets have a slight molasses flavour and are light and fluffy. I like them with maple syrup, or jam and Cashew Whipped Cream (page 181) for dessert.

250g silken tofu
1 cup self-raising flour
1 cup buckwheat flour
2 tsp. baking powder
1 ½ cups rice or soy milk
1 tbsp. blackstrap molasses
1 tsp. vanilla extract

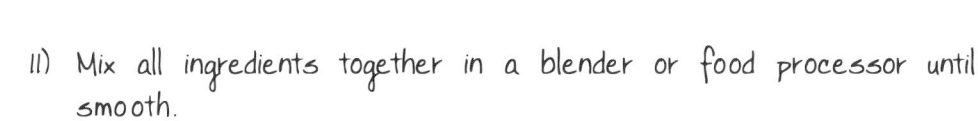

1) Mix all ingredients together in a blender or food processor until smooth.
2) Leave to stand for 30 minutes. The mixture will be quite thick, but that is okay as this makes thick, fluffy pikelets.
3) Heat a nonstick frying pan and grease with a little oil or vegan margarine.
4) Put spoonfuls of mixture into the pan and flip once bubbles start to pop on top of the batter. Cook until golden brown on both sides.
5) Serve at any temperature with your favourite topping.

There was a party on the kitchen table and everyone was invited!

Pancakes

Makes 6 standard-size pancakes

Thanks to the tofu, you would not know these pancakes are made without egg.

creative tip — Use the same mixture to make pikelets. Add cinnamon and brown sugar to make cinnamon pancakes or add sliced banana to the top of the pancake mixture while it is cooking for banana pancakes.

250g silken tofu
2 cups self-raising flour
1 ½ cups rice or soy milk
2 tbsp. maple syrup
2 tsp. baking powder

1) Mix all ingredients together in a blender or food processor until smooth.
2) Leave to stand for 30 minutes. The mixture will be quite thick, but that is okay as this makes thick, fluffy pancakes.
3) Heat a nonstick frying pan and grease with a little oil or vegan margarine.
4) Pour mixture into the pan and flip once bubbles start to pop on top of the batter. Cook until golden brown on both sides.
5) Serve at any temperature with your favourite pancake topping

Luxurious Fruit Salad

Serves 3-4

This fruit salad contains a small selection of fruits I believe are made to go together. Admittedly they are not the most economical fruits, but if you feel like splurging, and it is the right season, try this combination.

2 large passionfruit
1 large, peeled kiwifruit
½ sweet pineapple
1 large, ripe mango
1 punnet of strawberries

1) Scoop passionfruit into a medium-sized mixing bowl.
2) Cut all remaining fruits into bite-sized pieces and add to the bowl.
3) Mix well and serve.

drift away in a fruity heaven

Breakfast Smoothie

Serves 2

This smoothie is sweet, filling and healthy. It is suitable for breakfast, as a snack throughout the day or even as a dessert. Thanks to the tofu, you would never know that it does not contain ice cream.

½ cup rice or soy milk
6 large strawberries
1 frozen banana
½ tsp. vanilla extract
300g chilled silken tofu

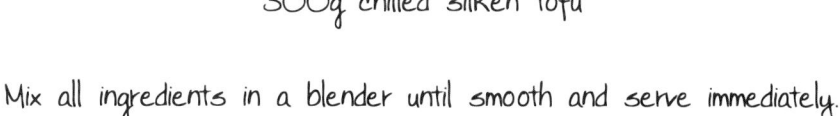

Mix all ingredients in a blender until smooth and serve immediately.

Fruit Slush

Serves 2

This refreshing drink can be enjoyed any time of day, but is especially good first thing on a summer's morning, preferably drunk whilst lounging in a deck chair.

2 cups fresh apple juice
5 fresh mint leaves
1 cup frozen fresh pineapple
1 cup frozen berries
(strawberries or blackberries)

Mix all ingredients in a blender until smooth and serve immediately.

"When a man wants to murder a tiger, he calls it sport; when a tiger wants to murder him, he calls it ferocity."
Pythagoras

Snacks

Snacks, Sides & Starters

"Gastronomy, has been the joy of all peoples through the ages. It produces beauty and wit and goes hand in hand with goodness of heart and a consideration of others."
Charles Pierre Monselet (1825-88) French journalist and author.

Riviera Burgers

Makes 10-12

I created these burgers whilst living on the French Riviera, although they are not inspired by the cheesy, meaty French cuisine. They are extremely versatile, and as well as being used as a burger, can also be served as a meal with salad or other vegetables. My favourite way to eat them is with roast vegetables and Cashew Pepper Gravy (page 142). When I make these I usually double the mixture and freeze the leftovers.

1¼ cups red lentils
1 tbsp. olive oil
2 spring onions, finely chopped
2 tbsp. fresh grated ginger
2 cloves garlic, crushed
2 tsp. ground cumin
2 cups grated sweet potato
500ml water
1 vegetable stock cube
½ tbsp. tamari sauce
100g breadcrumbs
1 cup fresh chopped coriander
olive oil for pan frying

1) Rinse lentils until the water runs clear and set aside.
2) In a medium-sized saucepan, heat the olive oil and then fry the spring onions until tender.
3) Add ginger, garlic and cumin and stir for one minute.
4) Add the sweet potato and simmer for 5 minutes, stirring often. Add a little of the water if it starts to stick.
5) Add water, stock cube, and tamari sauce. Stir until the stock cube is dissolved.
6) Add lentils and bring mixture to the boil.
7) Reduce heat and simmer, stirring often for approximately 15 minutes, or until lentils are very soft.
8) Remove from heat and place in a large mixing bowl. Leave to cool for 1 hour.
9) Add the breadcrumbs and coriander to the lentil mixture, then form the mixture into small patties.
10) Pan-fry the patties on both sides, in olive oil, until brown.

Summer Rice Burgers

Makes 7-8 large burgers or 12 small patties

These are really a summer treat as they are light and go beautifully with salad on a wholemeal roll. Top them off with some Sweet Chilli Sauce.

½ cup brown rice (uncooked)
½ cup rolled oats
1 tsp. dried thyme
1 tsp. ground cumin
125g silken tofu
2 cloves garlic, crushed
1 tbsp. tamari sauce
2 tbsp. natural tomato sauce
2 tsp. Dijon mustard
3 spring onions, finely chopped
½ cup oat bran
½ cup grated carrot
½ cup grated celery
¼ cup sesame seeds
Freshly ground black pepper, to season
Olive oil for pan frying

1) Put brown rice on to boil, and cook until very tender (for directions on how to cook brown rice, see page 23).
2) Meanwhile, place rolled oats into a medium-sized mixing bowl and add the thyme and cumin. Mix well.
3) Mash the tofu with a fork and add to the oats with garlic, tamari sauce, tomato sauce, mustard and spring onions. Stir well. By now the mixture should look very pasty.
4) Once the rice is cooked, either leave to cool or rinse through a strainer under cold water. Press all the water from rinsed rice. This is very important, otherwise the mixture will be too wet.
5) Add the rice, with the oat bran to the tofu mixture. Mix until well combined.
6) Add the carrot, celery, sesame seeds and pepper.
7) Form mixture into balls and then press down into a greased frying pan.
8) Pan fry on both sides until golden brown.

Mexican Patties

Makes 15

If you love the flavours of Mexican food, then you will love these. They are best served with Tomato Salsa (page 148), Refreshing Guacamole (page 150) and salad. They may be eaten as they are, or wrapped in a tortilla.

1 cup dried pinto beans (3 cups cooked)
1 small grated onion
1 tbsp. olive oil
3 cloves garlic, crushed
1 tsp. ground paprika
1 tbsp. ground cumin
1 tbsp. yellow mustard seeds
¼ tsp. ground nutmeg
1 tsp. dried oregano
½ tsp. sea salt
2 tbsp. lime juice
3 tbsp. tomato paste
¼ cup fresh finely chopped coriander
1½ cups water
½ cup polenta
1 cup breadcrumbs
olive oil for pan frying

1) If you are using dried pinto beans, prepare them according to directions on page 16.
2) In a small saucepan, stir fry onion in olive oil until tender.
3) Remove from heat, and add garlic and spices.
4) Return to heat and stir fry for one minute. Once done, leave to stand.
5) Puree beans in a food processor and then place into a mixing bowl with the onion and spice mixture.
6) Add the oregano, salt, lime juice, tomato paste and coriander. Mix well.
7) Put water into a small saucepan and bring to boil.
8) Add polenta and stir 3–4 minutes until the mixture thickens.
9) Quickly add the polenta to the bean mixture and stir until well combined.
10) Leave to sit for 10 minutes.
11) Add breadcrumbs gradually and mix well.
12) Form mixture into patties and pan fry in olive oil until browned on both sides. Serve hot or cold.

Spicy Potato Patties

Makes 10-12

These patties are quite spicy and are a great change to the usual mashed or roasted potatoes. It is preferable to make the mashed potato at least a couple of hours before so that it becomes firmer and easier to handle. They can be served with your main dish or can be eaten as a light meal with salad.

5 medium-sized potatoes (approx. 750g)
2 spring onions, finely chopped
1 tbsp. olive oil
1 large green chilli, seeded and finely chopped
3 cloves garlic, crushed
¼ cup fresh finely chopped coriander
¼ cup fresh finely chopped parsley
½ cup breadcrumbs
½ tsp. sea salt
olive oil for pan frying

1) Peel, steam and mash the potatoes, then leave to cool in a large mixing bowl.
2) In a small saucepan, stir fry spring onions in olive oil until tender.
3) Add chilli and garlic, and stir for one minute.
4) Remove from heat and add to the potatoes with the remaining ingredients (except olive oil). Mix until well combined.
5) Shape into patties and pan fry in olive oil until golden brown on both sides.

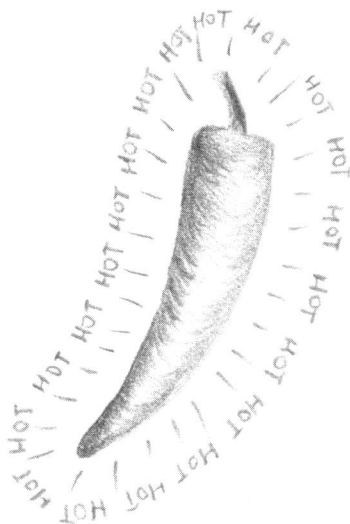

Moorish Lentil Balls

Makes 18-20

These delicious little snacks are perfect for party hors d'oeuvre, or for a healthy snack between meals, as they are baked rather than fried. They are flavoured with Indian spices and are best served with the Mint Dipping Sauce on page 147.

1 cup red lentils
1 small onion, grated
1 tbsp. olive oil
1 tbsp. fresh grated ginger
1 tsp. ground coriander
2 tsp. ground cumin
1 tsp. turmeric
1 tsp. garam masala
2 cloves garlic, crushed
½ tsp. sea salt
juice of ½ lemon
1 cup breadcrumbs

1) Prepare lentils according to directions on page 20.
2) Meanwhile, stir fry onion in olive oil until tender.
3) Remove from heat and add ginger, spices and garlic. Return to low heat, stirring constantly for 1 minute.
4) Add spice mixture to lentils, along with the salt and lemon juice. Mix until well combined.
5) Pre-heat the oven to 180°C.
6) When mixture is cool enough to touch, add the breadcrumbs and mix to an even consistency.
7) Form into small balls and place on a well greased oven tray.
8) Bake for 10-15 minutes (until crispy on the outside). Serve warm or cold.

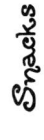

More please!

Mexican Bites

Makes 25-30

These are a small, flavoursome snack filled with the tastes of Mexico. I find they are great at parties served with Refreshing Guacamole (page 150) or as a sandwich filler with salad and Tomato Salsa (page 148).

1 cup dried chickpeas (2½ cups cooked)
2 spring onions, roughly chopped
2 tbsp. tomato paste
1 green capsicum, roughly chopped
2 cloves garlic, crushed
1 small green chilli, seeded and chopped
1 tbsp. ground cumin
1 tsp. dried oregano
Pinch of sea salt
freshly ground black pepper, to season
½ cup fresh finely chopped coriander
½ cup wholemeal flour

1) If you are using dried chickpeas, prepare them according to directions on page 19.
2) In a food processor, blend the chickpeas, spring onions, tomato paste, capsicum, garlic and chilli until smooth.
3) Pre-heat oven to 180°C.
4) Put mixture into a medium-sized mixing bowl and add all remaining ingredients except the flour.
5) Mix well, and then gradually add the flour.
6) Form mixture into small balls and place onto a greased baking tray.
7) Bake for 15-20 minutes, until crispy on the outside.
8) Serve warm or chilled.

Japanese Rice Balls

Makes approximately 25

Rice balls are a popular macrobiotic snack and are delicious and healthy at any time. I love to eat them with salad for lunch. They are best served with the Asian Dipping Sauce on page 147.

½ cup brown rice (uncooked)
1 tbsp. miso
1 cup water
1 cup rolled oats
¼ tsp. sea salt
½ tsp. ground ginger
125g silken tofu
1 tbsp. tamari sauce
3 tbsp. tahini
½ cup grated carrot
½ cup grated celery
¼ cup sesame seeds
¼ cup sunflower seeds

1) In a small saucepan, cover rice and miso with water.
2) Bring to the boil and stir until miso is dissolved, then leave to simmer until rice is tender (25–30 minutes). By this time, all water should be absorbed.
3) Once rice is cooked, leave to cool (or put into the refrigerator).
4) Meanwhile, place rolled oats into a medium-sized mixing bowl and add the salt and ginger. Mix well.
5) Mash in the tofu with a fork, and then add the tamari sauce and tahini. Stir until well combined.
6) Rice balls may be either baked or fried. If you intend to bake them, pre-heat the oven to 180°C.
7) Once the rice is cool, add to the tofu mixture with the remaining ingredients. Mix well. The mixture should be very firm and pasty.
8) Form mixture into small balls. To bake, place onto a greased baking tray and cook for 10–15 minutes, until brown and crispy.
9) To deep fry, heat vegetable oil and drop balls into the oil. Fry until golden brown.
10) Serve warm or chilled.

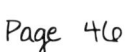

Crumbed Tofu Schnitzels

It is definitely possible to crumb food without using eggs. Soy flour has sufficient binding properties to hold everything together, as you will see when you make these yummy, marinated strips of tofu. Use them as a meat replacer in a meal or put them on sandwiches.

275g firm tofu
1 cup apple juice
2 tbsp. tamari sauce
½ tbsp. tabasco sauce
½ tbsp. balsamic vinegar
2 cloves garlic, crushed
1 tbsp. fresh grated ginger
½ cup soy milk
¼ cup soy flour
¾ cup plain flour
1 cup bread crumbs
Vegetable oil for frying

1) Cut the tofu into strips (the thickness is up to you).
2) In a bowl, combine the apple juice, tamari sauce, Tabasco sauce, balsamic vinegar, garlic and ginger.
3) Add the tofu strips and stir to coat.
4) Cover and refrigerate for at least 2 hours. Mix them up a couple of times to ensure that all of the strips absorb the flavours of the marinade.
5) Once the tofu strips are ready, whisk the soy milk and soy flour in a small mixing bowl.
6) Spread the plain flour onto a dinner plate and do the same with the breadcrumbs on a separate plate.
7) Coat each tofu strip in flour, dip into the soy milk mixture, and then coat in bread crumbs.
8) Pan fry the strips in vegetable oil until golden brown on each side.
9) Serve hot with your meal or cold as a sandwich filler.

Not-Sausage Rolls

Makes 40 party-size rolls

These are a great little party snack.

creative tip: Fresh herbs, vegetables or soy cheese can be added to the mixture. You can also use your own pastry if you don't like the frozen kind.

1 cup TVP
1 cup boiling water
½ cup peanuts
½ onion, grated
½ tbsp. olive oil
2 tsp. dried mixed herbs
½ cup breadcrumbs
1 tbsp. tamari sauce
½ cup apple juice
pepper to season
3 sheets puff pastry

1) Pre-heat the oven to 180°C.
2) Put TVP into a glass or metal mixing bowl and pour boiling water over the top. Leave to stand for 5 minutes.
3) Meanwhile, put peanuts into a blender or food processor and mix until they are the consistency of fine grains.
4) Add peanuts with remaining ingredients (except pastry) to the TVP. Mix well.
5) Cut pastry sheets in half and lay a generous amount of mixture down one side, leaving a 1-2cm edge. Press the mixture together into a sausage shape.
6) Wet the small edge and then roll pastry over to encase the mixture.
7) Cut into small rolls (they should resemble party sausage rolls) and place onto an ungreased baking tray.
8) Bake for 25-30 minutes until pastry is golden and serve warm with tomato sauce.

Tortilla Sandwiches

Makes 4 large sandwiches

These may be served for lunch or as a light evening meal. They combine ingredients that are bursting with freshness and flavour.

2 medium-sized tomatoes (approx. 300g)
¾ cup fresh finely chopped coriander
2 medium-sized avocados
2 limes
1 red onion, finely chopped
1 tbsp. olive oil
3 tsp. ground cumin
500g sweet potato, peeled and diced small
2 cloves garlic, crushed
1½ cups corn kernels
4 large flour tortillas

1) Dice the tomatoes and place into a mixing bowl with the coriander.
2) Mash the avocado with the juice from 1 lime and then add to the mixing bowl. Set aside.
3) Stir fry the onion in olive oil until tender.
4) Add the ground cumin and mix for one minute.
5) Add the sweet potato, garlic, corn and the juice from the remaining lime. Mix well.
6) Cover the pan and cook over medium heat until the sweet potato is tender. Stir often to stop the food sticking.
7) Sandwiches may be baked in the oven, pan fried or grilled on both sides until brown and crispy. If you intend baking them, pre-heat the oven to 180°C.
8) Combine the sweet potato mixture with the other ingredients in the mixing bowl.
9) Spoon the filling onto half of each tortilla, then fold each one over to form a semicircle. Proceed with your preferred method of cooking, then serve hot with a salad.

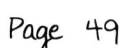

Vegetable Curry Parcels

Makes approximately 20

These snacks are made with a healthy rye pastry that is crunchy and delicious. They are best served with Sweet Chilli Sauce.

creative tip: This recipe is as versatile as you want to make it. Vary the vegetables or the spices to create totally different flavours. You can even use a pizza sauce to bind the vegetables so that the parcels have an italian flavour!

Filling
3 cloves garlic, crushed
1 tbsp. lemon juice
1 tbsp. fresh grated ginger
a pinch of cayenne pepper
1 tsp. garam masala
1 tsp. ground coriander
½ tsp. sea salt
2 medium-sized potatoes (approx. 300g)
2 medium-sized carrots (approx. 200g)
100g peeled pumpkin
100g broccoli and/or cauliflower florets
1 onion, finely chopped
2 tsp. cumin seeds
1 tbsp. olive oil
3 tbsp. tomato paste

Pastry
1¼ cups warm water
3 cups rye flour
¾ cup wholemeal plain flour
¼ tsp. sea salt
3 tbsp. vegan margarine
¼ cup olive oil (for basting)

1) Combine garlic, lemon juice, ginger, cayenne pepper, garam masala, ground coriander and salt in a small bowl and set aside.
2) Cut all vegetables into very small pieces (except onion), keeping the broccoli/cauliflower separate.

3) In a large saucepan, stir fry onion and cumin seeds in olive oil.
4) Once onion is tender, add the lemon and spice mixture and stir well for one minute.
5) Add the chopped vegetables (except for broccoli/cauliflower) and tomato paste, and simmer, stirring often until tender. Add a couple of tablespoons of water at this stage to prevent the vegetables sticking to the bottom of the pan.
6) While the vegetables are cooking, make the pastry. Place warm water into a mixing bowl and add the flours and sea salt.
7) Mix well into a firm dough and then add the margarine.
8) At this point, pre-heat the oven to 180°C.
9) Stir the dough and then place onto a floured surface and knead for approximately 5 minutes, (until the dough is well combined and manageable).
10) Roll the dough out on a floured board until it is about 2 millimetres thick and then cut into rounds with a cookie cutter, round glass or bottle top. You can make them any size you like, but as a guide, I would suggest 7-8cm in diameter.
11) Remove the vegetables from heat and stir in the broccoli/cauliflower. It doesn't need to be cooked now because the time in the oven will cook it perfectly.
12) Spoon the vegetable mixture into the centre of each pastry round, then pinch the edges together over the top so it forms a pasty shape.
13) Place onto a greased baking tray and brush lightly with olive oil.
14) Bake for 20-25 minutes or until the parcels are crispy.

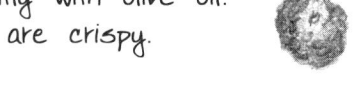

Curry in a Hurry!

Savoury Scrolls

Makes 20

These scrolls are a savoury snack, delicious served warm.

creative tip: The fillings in these little scrolls can be varied in countless ways. Your favourite pizza toppings, olives or mushrooms are a few examples.

1 onion, finely chopped
1 tbsp. olive oil
2 medium-sized tomatoes (approx. 300g), pureed
2 cloves garlic, crushed
4 tbsp. tomato paste
3 cups self-raising flour
pinch of sea salt
45g vegan margarine
1 cup soy milk
170g finely chopped spinach
1½-2 cups grated soy cheese

1) In a small saucepan, stir fry the onion in olive oil until tender.
2) Add the tomatoes, garlic and tomato paste and simmer for 15 minutes.
3) Remove from heat and set aside.
4) Meanwhile, pre-heat the oven to 180°C and grease two baking trays.
5) Place flour and salt into a large mixing bowl.
6) Cut the margarine into chunks and rub into the flour with fingertips until the mixture resembles breadcrumbs.
7) Add the soy milk and combine until the mixture can be rolled into a dough.
8) Knead dough for 5 minutes and then roll out on a floured surface so that it is 2mm thick and in a large square shape. (It will require quite a lot of rolling). Cut the dough down the centre to form two long rectangles.
9) Spread a layer of tomato sauce over each of the rectangles but leave one of the long ends uncovered about 1cm from the edge.

10) Spread the spinach evenly over the top, followed by the cheese.
11) Roll the dough across the width so that it becomes a long sausage shaped coil. When you get to the end, brush the uncovered end with water so that it sticks together and holds the sausage shape.
12) Cut the coil at 5cm intervals.
13) Place scrolls onto the baking tray and brush the top with olive oil.
14) Bake for 15-20 minutes.
15) Serve warm with vegan margarine or as they are.

Snacks

Spring Rolls

Makes 10-12 large rolls

Spring rolls are one of my favourite Asian dishes. The best thing is you can vary the filling to suit your tastes. Don't be daunted by the pastry either. Once you get the hang of it you will find it easy. They are delicious served with Sweet Chilli Sauce.

150g rice vermicelli
1 large carrot, grated (approx. 180g)
1 small zucchini, grated (approx. 150g)
2 tbsp. fresh grated ginger
2 cloves garlic, crushed
3 tbsp. tamari sauce
¼ cup fresh finely chopped coriander
1 tbsp. arrowroot
3 tbsp. water
10-12 spring roll wrappers
vegetable oil for frying

1) Boil vermicelli for a short time until just tender (3-4 minutes) and set aside to drain.
2) In a mixing bowl, combine carrot, zucchini, ginger, garlic, tamari sauce and coriander.
3) Chop vermicelli roughly and add to the mixture. Mix well.
4) Combine the arrowroot and water in a small dish and set aside.
5) Spoon mixture onto wrappers close to the middle, and on the diagonal. (See information below for rolling tips).
6) Brush arrowroot mixture onto edges of pastry and then roll, folding edges over to seal the mixture in.
7) Deep or shallow fry in vegetable oil until brown and serve hot.

Rolling spring rolls is very easy once you get the hang of it. Note these handy tips:
- Make sure wrappers are fully defrosted.
- If the pastry sheets don't separate well, wet a clean cloth, wring it out and lay it over the pastry so that the moisture soaks in just enough to lift the top sheet.
- Make sure the mixture is not too wet. It may be necessary to press excess moisture from it with clean hands.
- Roll on a diagonal so that the final edge is only small.

Oven Chips

Serves 4 as a side

Deep fried chips are delicious but extremely high in fat. Try this oven-baked alternative.

creative tip: Vary the herbs and spices to your liking. Try using sweet potatoes for a variation too, and serve them with Sweet Chilli Sauce.

4 medium-sized potatoes (approx. 600g)
1 tbsp. olive oil
1 tsp. ground paprika
1 tsp. dried mixed herbs
½ tsp. sea salt

1) Pre-heat oven to 180°C.
2) Scrub potatoes and then slice into chips.
3) In a large mixing bowl, toss the chips with the olive oil.
4) Add the remaining ingredients and mix until chips are evenly coated.
5) Arrange chips onto two baking trays and bake for 30-35 minutes (cooking time will vary depending on the thickness of your chips).

Karelien Potato Pies

Makes 18

These pies are adapted from a traditional Finnish recipe that ordinarily contains a filling of creamed rice or plain mashed potato. I have added a few other flavours to make them tastier.

Filling
5 medium-sized potatoes, peeled (approx. 750g)
2 sprigs fresh rosemary
1 spring onion
3 tbsp. fresh parsley, finely chopped
2 cloves garlic, crushed
5 tbsp. soy or rice milk
½ tsp. sea salt
freshly ground black pepper, to season

Pastry
½ cup warm water
1 cup rye flour
¼ cup wholemeal plain flour
1 tbsp. vegan margarine
¼ cup olive oil (for basting)

1) Cut potatoes into quarters and steam until very tender.
2) Meanwhile, chop the rosemary leaves and spring onion very finely.
3) Once the potatoes are soft, place them into a large mixing bowl and mash until all large lumps are gone.
4) Add the remaining filling ingredients and mix well.
5) To make the pastry, place warm water into a mixing bowl and add the flours.
6) Mix well into a firm dough and then knead in the margarine.
7) At this point, pre-heat the oven to 220°C.
8) Place the dough onto a floured surface and knead for approximately 5 minutes (until the dough is well combined and manageable).
9) Roll the dough out until it is 2–3 millimetres thick, and then cut into rounds with a cookie cutter, round glass or bottle top. You can make them any size you like, but as a guide, I would suggest 7–8cm in diameter.

10) Roll each round into a paper-thin oval, taking care not to break the pastry. The rye flour makes the mixture quite tough, but you will still need to take some care.
11) Place a thin layer of the filling down the centre of the oval, leaving 1-2 centimetres all round the edges.
12) Once done, start at the bottom and simultaneously pinch the pastry up over the filling on both sides, finishing at the top.
13) Place pies onto a greased tray and brush with olive oil.
14) Bake for 10-12 minutes (until brown) and serve warm or cold as a snack.

Snacks

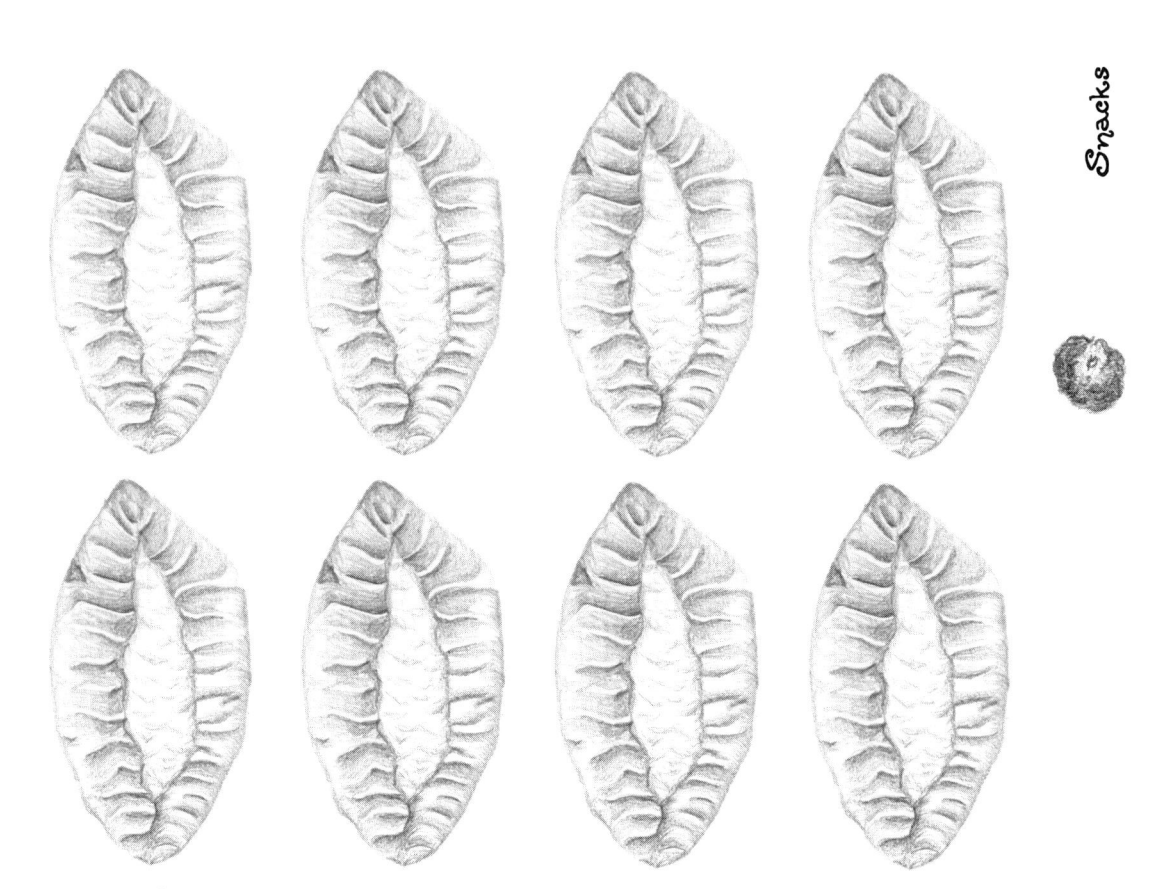

It really is quite easy once you get the hang of it!

Mixed Vegetable Bake

Serves 4-5 as a side

For those nights when you want to make something quick and easy but still healthy, try this as a meal. This dish is also great as a side of vegetables to go with your main meal.

2 cloves garlic, crushed
1 tbsp. fresh grated ginger
1 tbsp. fenugreek seeds
1 tbsp. fennel seeds
2 tsp. yellow mustard seeds
1 tsp. turmeric
3 tbsp. olive oil
3 medium-sized potatoes (approx. 450g), scrubbed
400g sweet potato, peeled
2 large carrots (approx. 360g), scrubbed
2 medium-sized tomatoes (approx. 300g), diced
½ tsp. sea salt
5 dried apricots, chopped finely
2 tbsp. ketjap manis (Indonesian soy sauce)
2 tightly packed cups of roughly chopped English spinach

1) Pre-heat oven to 180°C.
2) In a small saucepan, cook garlic, ginger and spices in 1 tbsp. of olive oil for 1 minute. Stir constantly and then remove from heat and set aside.
3) Cut potatoes, sweet potatoes and carrots into bite size pieces.
4) Pour vegetables into a large baking dish and stir in all remaining ingredients excluding the spinach.
5) Bake for 45-50 minutes (cooking time will vary according to size of vegetable pieces).
6) When the potato pieces are golden outside and soft inside, stir in the spinach and serve.

Carrots & Beans in Tomato Zest

Serves 4 as a side

Looking for a more interesting way to eat carrots and beans? I was, and I came up with this dish of sweet and slightly sour vegetables. If you really enjoy the sauce, you could add other vegetables and make it into a meal by serving it with rice.

1 medium-sized tomato, diced (approx. 150g)
1 clove garlic, crushed
¼ cup apple juice
1 tsp. fresh grated ginger
½ tbsp. tamari sauce
½ tbsp. rice mirin
1 medium-sized carrot, sliced (approx. 100g)
1½ cups chopped green beans

1) Put all ingredients except carrot and beans into a small saucepan.
2) Simmer over medium heat until the tomato becomes mushy.
3) Add the carrot and simmer for a few minutes.
4) Add beans and cook a further 3-4 minutes then serve.

Rosemary & Lime Potatoes

Serves 4-5 as a side

One of my favourites, I make this as a side, or a light meal.

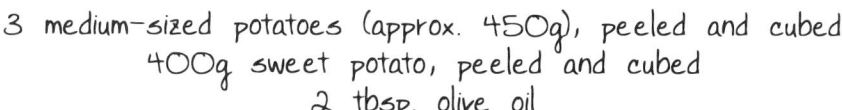

3 medium-sized potatoes (approx. 450g), peeled and cubed
400g sweet potato, peeled and cubed
2 tbsp. olive oil
2 cloves garlic, crushed
1 tbsp. tamari sauce
1 tbsp. lime juice
2 sprigs fresh rosemary

1) Steam potatoes and sweet potatoes until they are just tender.
2) Heat the oil in a frying pan, then add cooked potatoes (plain and sweet).
3) Stir fry until they start to brown then stir in the remaining ingredients. The dish is ready when the potatoes are soft.

Pumpkin & Sweet Potato Fusion

Serves 4 as a side

This dish uses the natural sweetness of pumpkin and sweet potato to contrast with spices and coriander. Serve as a light meal or as a side dish to provide flavour and plenty of colour to your meal.

2 tbsp. olive oil
2 tbsp. tamari sauce
1 tbsp. balsamic vinegar
2 tbsp. fresh grated ginger
2 tsp. curry powder
3 cloves garlic, crushed
1 onion, sliced into rings
400g sweet potato, peeled and sliced
400g pumpkin, peeled and sliced
½ cup fresh finely chopped coriander

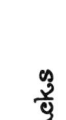

1) Pre-heat oven to 180°C.
2) In a small mixing bowl, combine olive oil, tamari sauce, balsamic vinegar, ginger, curry powder and garlic.
3) Place the onion, sweet potato and pumpkin, into a large baking dish and combine with the sauce ingredients.
4) Bake for 35-40 minutes (cooking time will vary according to size of vegetable pieces).
5) When vegetables are soft, stir through the coriander and serve.

Hazelnutty Beans

Serves 4-5 as a side

Hazelnuts give these beans that extra boost they need to make them more interesting and delicious.

600g green beans
50g hazelnuts
1 tsp. black peppercorns
2 tbsp. tamari sauce
4 tbsp. fresh finely chopped parsley

1) Steam beans until just tender (approximately 5 minutes).
2) Meanwhile, crush hazelnuts in a food processor until they are in tiny pieces.
3) Dry roast the hazelnuts in a small saucepan until they are browned then set aside.
4) Crush black peppercorns in a mortar and pestle, or if you don't have one, grind in a pepper grinder.
5) Once beans are ready, place into a serving dish and toss with remaining ingredients.

Mekong Asparagus

This asparagus dish has an Asian flavour and goes well with roasted vegetables. Make sure that you adapt the cooking time to the thickness of your spears so that they are cooked until just tender.

200g fresh asparagus
¼ cup apple juice
1 tbsp. tamari sauce
1 tbsp. rice mirin
1 tsp. fresh grated ginger
1 clove garlic, crushed

1) Pre-heat oven to 180°C.
2) In a small baking dish, combine all ingredients.
3) Bake for 15 minutes, stirring at 5 minute intervals (if you use fine asparagus spears, reduce the cooking time to 7 minutes).

Salads

"If slaughterhouses had glass walls, everyone would be a vegetarian."
Paul McCartney

Salads

"All flesh is grass and its beauty is like the flowers in the field."
Isaiah 40:6

Tomato Salsa Salad

This is my favourite salad to take to barbecues. Vary the chilli factor as little or as much as you like.

1 small red onion, finely chopped
1 banana capsicum, finely chopped
1 red capsicum, diced
5 medium-sized tomatoes, diced (approx. 650g)
2 cloves garlic, crushed
½ cup fresh finely chopped coriander
½ cup fresh finely chopped parsley
1 tsp. ground cumin
1 tbsp. balsamic vinegar
1 small red chilli, seeded and finely chopped

1) Place all ingredients into a salad bowl and mix well.
2) Serve garnished with a sprig of parsley.

Italian Salad

Instead of using lettuce in this salad, I use watercress, spinach and rocket leaves which lend a stronger flavour. The bright colours and balsamic dressing, make it an attractive and delicious accompaniment to meals at dinner parties and barbecues.

100g mix of watercress, English spinach and rocket leaves
1 red capsicum, cut into strips
½ red onion, cut into rings
4–5 small radishes, sliced
200g cherry tomatoes
2 tbsp. olive oil
1 tbsp. balsamic vinegar
1 tsp. dried oregano
freshly ground black pepper, to season

1) Place the greens, capsicum, onion, radishes and tomatoes into a large salad bowl and toss until well mixed.
2) In a separate, smaller bowl, prepare the dressing by combining the remaining ingredients.
3) Toss through the vegetables and serve.

Wild Rice Salad

This is a tasty salad that includes raw vegetables, wild and brown rice, and a zesty dressing. I like to serve it with a garden salad and some type of burger or patty (see the Snacks, Sides and Starters section beginning on page 39 for a range of ideas).

1 cup brown rice
½ cup wild rice
1 cinnamon stick
1 spring onion, finely chopped
1 red capsicum, finely chopped
1 cup grated zucchini
1 cup grated carrot
1 tbsp. fresh grated ginger
juice of ½ a lemon
1 tbsp. rice mirin
1 tbsp. tamari sauce
1 tsp. dried mixed herbs
3 tbsp. cold pressed olive oil
freshly ground black pepper, to season
¼ cup roasted sesame seeds

1) Put both rices on to boil in the same pot, at the same time with the cinnamon stick. Cook until both grains are very soft (for more detailed directions on cooking brown rice, see page 23).
2) When the rice is cooked, leave to cool.
3) Once the rice is cool, place into a mixing bowl and add all vegetables including ginger. Mix well.
4) In a small bowl make the dressing by combining the lemon juice, rice mirin, tamari sauce, mixed herbs and olive oil.
5) Add the dressing, pepper and sesame seeds to the rice and mix until well combined.
6) Serve as a light meal or with other salads.

Refreshing Bean Boost

This tasty salad has the bulk of beans, as well as a good mixture of raw vegetables. It is a great accompaniment to a Mexican meal, but also goes well with a barbecue.

½ cup red kidney beans (1½ cups cooked)
½ large cucumber, diced
4 medium-sized tomatoes, diced (approx. 600g)
1 red capsicum, diced
2 spring onions, finely chopped
1 cup fresh finely chopped coriander
1 cup corn kernels
3 tbsp. water
1 tbsp. balsamic vinegar
Juice of ½ lime
1 tbsp. natural tomato sauce
1 tsp. ground cumin
½ tsp. freshly ground black pepper
2 cloves garlic, crushed

1) If you are using dried kidney beans, prepare them according to directions on page 17, then set aside to cool.
2) Place cucumber, tomatoes, capsicum, spring onions, coriander and corn kernels into a large salad bowl.
3) Add the cooled kidney beans and mix until well combined.
4) In a small bowl, mix the remaining ingredients and then stir through the salad.
5) Serve chilled.

Mitchell's Red Salad

The colour of this salad is amazing and it needs no dressing thanks to the sweetness of the beetroot.

1 small head of cos lettuce (or any other dark green variety)
1 capsicum, thinly sliced
½ large or 1 small cucumber, diced
250g shredded red cabbage
1 cup grated, raw beetroot
2 tbsp. nori flakes
1 large carrot (approx. 180g)

1) Roughly chop the lettuce and place into a large salad bowl.
2) Add the capsicum, cucumber, cabbage, beetroot and nori flakes.
3) Using a peeler, shred the carrot into the salad and toss until well combined.

Sesame Salad

Don't be fooled into thinking that this salad is not worthwhile due to its extreme simplicity... It is one of my favourite salads to make because it is so full of flavour and so easy!

½ cup sesame seeds
1 large carrot, sliced (approx. 180g)
½ small cucumber, sliced
2 medium-sized tomatoes, cut into wedges (approx. 300g)
1 capsicum, cut into strips
2 handfuls of mixed lettuce leaves
Handful of mung bean sprouts

1) Place sesame seeds into a small, dry saucepan and roast over medium heat, moving them around often so they don't burn. Set aside.
2) Place remaining ingredients into a large salad bowl and mix well.
3) Place sesame seeds into a mortar and pestle if you have one and crush them. This is not essential but it does release more flavour and goodness from the sesame seeds.
4) Pour sesame seeds over the salad and toss well.

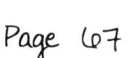

Mango & Avocado Salad

This is a refreshing summer salad that is wonderful on its own as a light meal or as an accompaniment to other salads.

½ head of dark green lettuce
1 large, ripe mango
½ medium-sized avocado
1 red capsicum, diced
½ cup diced cucumber
2 tbsp. chopped fresh mint
¼ cup desiccated coconut
¼ cup sunflower seeds
1 tbsp. cold pressed sunflower oil
1 tbsp. apple juice
1 tbsp. lemon juice

1) Break lettuce leaves into rough pieces and place into a large salad bowl.
2) Slice the side panels off the mango, following the grain of the seed. Carve into squares with a knife and then turn the skin out so that the pieces stand up.
3) Cut the mango pieces from the sides and the seed, and add to the lettuce.
4) Peel the avocado, dice and add to the bowl with the capsicum, cucumber, mint, coconut and sunflower seeds.
5) In a small bowl, combine the remaining ingredients and pour over the salad.
6) Toss until well combined and serve chilled.

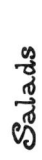

Indulge in the fruit of the gods!

Mostly Green Salad

This is a very light, healthy salad that goes well with pasta dishes. For the mixed green leaves, use a combination of any of the following: varieties of lettuce, mustard greens, baby spinach, chicory, watercress, rocket or chard.

120g mixed green leaves
½ cup sprouted mung beans
½ cup alfalfa sprouts
¼ cup finely chopped, rehydrated sun-dried tomatoes*
1 tbsp. cold pressed olive oil
½ tbsp. balsamic vinegar

* To rehydrate sun-dried tomatoes, soak them in boiling water for 5 minutes or use marinated ones.

1) Toss the mixed greens with the mung beans, alfalfa and sun-dried tomatoes until they are well mixed.
2) Drizzle with the olive oil and balsamic vinegar and mix again.

Try making your own alfalfa sprouts...
1) Soak alfalfa seeds in a sprouting bottle for at least 4 hours.
2) Rinse and leave bottle to stand upside down so the water can drain out. If you don't have a sprouting jar cover the top with some stocking or cheesecloth.
3) Rinse a couple of times a day until the sprouts are ready to eat (3-5 days). Sprouts will grow faster in summer and slower in winter.
4) Refrigerate for up to a week.

Roasted Vegetable & Couscous Salad

This salad is quite filling and usually only needs to be accompanied by a simple green salad. It has the delicious flavours of mint, parsley, cinnamon and lemon to compliment the roast vegetables, and may even be served warm as a light meal or side dish.

1 cup couscous
1 cup boiling water
1 tbsp. vegan margarine
1 cup very small cubes pumpkin
1 cup very small cubes eggplant
1 red capsicum, chopped into small pieces
½ tbsp. olive oil
½ tsp. sea salt
1 tbsp. cold pressed olive oil
1 tbsp. fresh lemon juice
½ tsp. ground cinnamon
1 tbsp. fresh finely chopped parsley
1 tbsp. fresh finely chopped mint

1) Pre-heat oven to 180°C.
2) Prepare couscous according to directions on page 23.
3) Place the pumpkin, eggplant and capsicum into a baking dish and drizzle with the olive oil and salt.
4) Mix well and bake for 20 minutes or until the vegetables start to char. Set aside to cool.
5) In a small dish, combine the remaining ingredients to make a dressing and stir into the couscous along with the cooled vegetables.
6) Serve chilled.

Mixed Seed Salad

This is a tasty, nutritious salad that has a wonderful flavour owing to the variety of roasted seeds.

1 tbsp. sesame seeds
1 tbsp. sunflower seeds
1 tbsp. linseeds/flaxseeds
2 tbsp. pumpkin seeds
2 handfuls of mixed lettuce leaves
½ small cucumber, sliced
1 capsicum, sliced
200g cherry tomatoes
Handful of alfalfa sprouts
1 large carrot (approx. 180g)
2 tbsp. cold pressed olive oil
2 tsp. balsamic vinegar

1) Place all seeds onto a baking tray and roast for 10 minutes at 180°C, or dry-roast in a frying pan until browned.
2) Place lettuce leaves, cucumber, capsicum, cherry tomatoes and alfalfa into a large salad bowl.
3) Shave the carrot into strips with a peeler and add to the bowl. Mix well.
4) Add the roasted seeds, olive oil and balsamic vinegar and toss until well combined.

Tomato & Basil Salad

Nothing beats the taste of tomato and basil. This very quick and easy salad takes advantage of the simplicity of this combination.

500g cherry tomatoes
½ cup chopped fresh basil leaves
1 tbsp. cold pressed olive oil
1 tbsp. balsamic vinegar

1) Combine all ingredients in a small salad bowl.
2) Serve chilled.

Soups

> "The time will come when men such as I will look upon the murder of animals as they now look on the murder of men."
> ***Leonardo da Vinci***

Soups

"Beautiful soup, so rich and green Waiting in a hot tureen!
Who for such dainties would not stoop? Soup of the evening, beautiful soup!."
Lewis Caroll, Alice in Wonderland

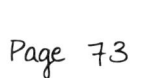

Carrot and Coriander Soup

Serves 4-5
This is a simple and tasty soup

1 average-sized bunch coriander
1 large onion, chopped
1 tbsp. olive oil
2 large cloves garlic, crushed
2 bay leaves
1 litre water
1 kg carrots, roughly chopped
pepper to season

1) Remove leaves from coriander stems and set aside, then roughly chop the stems.
2) Using a large saucepan or soup pot, fry onion in olive oil until tender.
3) Add the remaining ingredients (except coriander leaves) and bring to the boil.
4) Cover and reduce to simmer for 30 minutes, stirring often.
5) Once carrots are soft, remove the bay leaves and puree the soup with the coriander leaves. Season with pepper before serving.

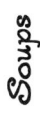

Middle Eastern Vegetable Soup

Serves 4-5

This is a light soup with many contrasting flavours that tingle your tongue. Don't feel that you have to stick to the vegetables I have used, although the tomatoes are a part of the Middle Eastern flavour so it is best to leave them in.

1 large onion, chopped
1 tbsp. olive oil
1 tsp. ground cumin
3 large cloves garlic, crushed
2 tbsp. fresh grated ginger
2 medium-sized carrots, diced (approx. 200g)
2 medium-sized potatoes, peeled and diced (approx. 300g)
4 medium-sized tomatoes, diced (approx. 600g)
3 cups water
½ tsp. freshly ground black pepper
2 tsp. balsamic vinegar
2 tbsp. tamari sauce
1 tbsp. savoury yeast flakes
½ cup fresh finely chopped coriander

1) Using a large saucepan or soup pot, stir fry onion in olive oil until tender.
2) Remove from heat and add cumin, garlic and ginger.
3) Return to heat and stir for 1 minute, being careful not to burn the ingredients.
4) Add carrots, potatoes, and tomatoes. Stir and simmer for 5 minutes.
5) Add remaining ingredients except yeast flakes and coriander. Bring to the boil.
6) Cover and simmer over medium/low heat for 30-40 minutes. Soup is done when potatoes are tender.
7) Before serving, stir in the yeast flakes and coriander.

Tomato and Basil Soup

Serves 4–5

This tomato soup is made with fresh ingredients. The apple juice cuts the bitterness of the tomatoes and gives the soup a sweet flavour that complements the basil nicely.

1 large onion, roughly chopped
1 tbsp. olive oil
6 medium-sized tomatoes, diced (approx. 900g)
2 large cloves garlic, crushed
1 cup apple juice
½ tbsp. balsamic vinegar
4 tbsp. tomato paste
1 cup water
sea salt/black pepper, to season
2 tightly packed cups fresh basil leaves

1) Using a large saucepan or soup pot, stir fry onion in olive oil, until tender.
2) Add tomatoes and garlic, and simmer for 5 minutes.
3) Add apple juice, vinegar, tomato paste and water, and simmer covered for 20 minutes.
4) Season with salt and pepper, and then puree in a blender or food processor with the basil.
5) When done, return to the pot and reheat before serving.

Shanta's Pumpkin Soup

Serves 4-5

Shanta is my aunty, and she created this delicious alternative to the usual pumpkin soup. When I think of Shanta what comes to mind is her happy accordion music, great food and lots of laughs. This is definitely worth sharing!

4 medium-sized carrots, (approx. 400g)
500g peeled pumpkin
300g peeled sweet potato
1 large onion, roughly chopped
2 tbsp. fresh grated ginger
4 cloves garlic, crushed
1 small red chilli, seeded and finely chopped
1 tbsp. olive oil
2½ cups water
1 tbsp. miso
1 tbsp. tamari sauce
½ cup coconut cream

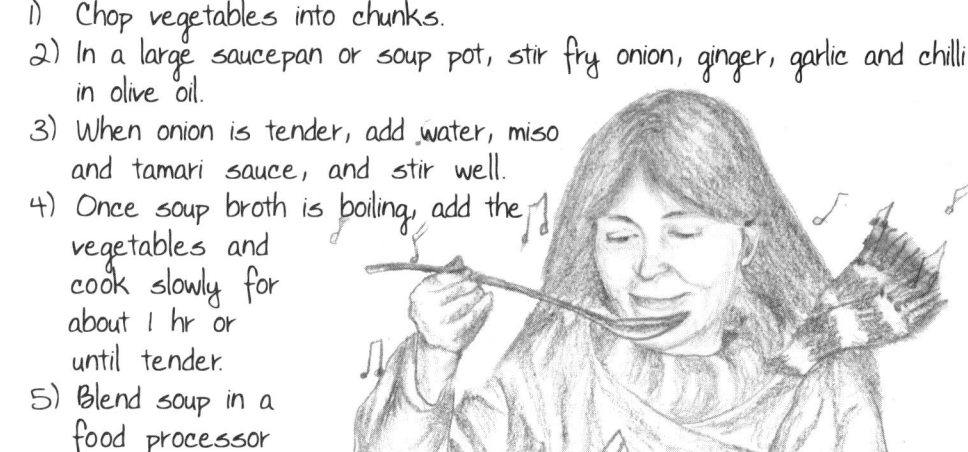

1) Chop vegetables into chunks.
2) In a large saucepan or soup pot, stir fry onion, ginger, garlic and chilli in olive oil.
3) When onion is tender, add water, miso and tamari sauce, and stir well.
4) Once soup broth is boiling, add the vegetables and cook slowly for about 1 hr or until tender.
5) Blend soup in a food processor with the coconut cream.
6) When done, return to the pot and reheat before serving.

Soups

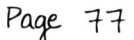

Thai Vegetable Soup

Serves 4

This soup is perfect for a cold night, with its delicious combination of root vegetables, coconut milk and chilli.

2 medium-sized potatoes, peeled (approx. 300g)
300g peeled sweet potato
300g peeled pumpkin
1 medium-sized carrot (approx. 100g)
1 red onion, finely chopped
1 tbsp. olive oil
2 cloves garlic, crushed
2 tbsp. fresh grated ginger
1 small red chilli, seeded and finely chopped
1 tsp. dried oregano
½ tsp. ground cinnamon
1 cup water
1 vegetable stock cube
200ml coconut cream/milk
½ cup fresh chopped coriander

1) Chop vegetables into bite size cubes.
2) Using a large saucepan or soup pot, stir fry onion in olive oil until tender.
3) Add garlic, ginger and chilli, and stir fry for one minute.
4) Add the vegetables, oregano and cinnamon, and mix well over the heat until vegetables are coated with the herbs and spices.
5) Add water and stock cube, and simmer soup for 20-25 minutes over medium heat, stirring often.
6) When vegetables are very soft, lower heat and add coconut cream/milk. Stir until well combined.
7) Remove from heat and stir in the coriander.

Tomato and Lentil Soup

Serves 4-5

The lentils in this soup make it a meal with plenty of protein and flavour. Serve it with a salad and some warm wholemeal bread.

creative tip: Add other vegetables or beans to this soup and vary the herbs to suit your tastes.

1 cup red lentils
1 finely chopped onion
1 tbsp. olive oil
5 medium-sized tomatoes, diced (approx. 750g)
3 cloves garlic, crushed
4 cups water
½ tsp. freshly ground black pepper
1 tsp. dried mixed herbs
3 tbsp. tomato paste
¼ cup fresh finely chopped parsley
½ tsp. sea salt

1) Rinse lentils until the water runs clear and set aside.
2) Using a large saucepan or soup pot, stir fry onion in olive oil until tender.
3) Add tomatoes and garlic, and simmer until tomatoes are soft and mushy.
4) Add water, pepper, mixed herbs, tomato paste and lentils, and mix well.
5) Simmer over medium heat until lentils become soft (about 20 minutes). Make sure you stir the soup often so that the lentils do not stick to the pan.
6) Before serving, stir in parsley and salt.

Wild Winter Warm-up

Serves 4-5

This soup is a healthy meal in itself due to the added bulk of the barley. I like to serve it with garlic bread and a salad.

½ cup pearl barley
1 large onion, diced
1 tbsp. olive oil
3 large cloves garlic, crushed
5 medium-sized tomatoes, diced (approx. 750g)
2 sticks of celery, diced
300g sweet potato, peeled and diced
1 large carrot (approx. 180g), chopped
1 vegetable stock cube
2 tbsp. tamari sauce
3 cups water
½ tsp. freshly ground black pepper
¼ cup fresh finely chopped parsley

1) Blanch the barley and set aside (see blanching directions on page 15).
2) Using a large saucepan or soup pot, stir fry the onion in olive oil until tender.
3) Add the remaining ingredients except the parsley. Mix well and cover.
4) Leave to simmer over low heat, stirring occasionally until the barley and potatoes are soft. This will take 25-30 minutes.
5) Remove from heat and stir in the parsley before serving.

Creamy Vegetable Soup

Serves 4-5

This is a simple, sweet soup flavoured with root vegetables and coconut milk.

1 large parsnip
1 swede
2 large carrots (approx. 360g)
2 medium-sized potatoes (approx. 300g)
1 small bunch fresh dill
1 medium-sized onion, roughly chopped
1 tbsp. olive oil
1 tbsp. fresh grated ginger
750ml water
½ vegetable stock cube
pepper to season
270ml coconut milk

1) Peel and roughly chop the vegetables.
2) Seperate the dill leaves from the stalks and keep both.
3) Using a large saucepan or soup pot, stir fry the onion in olive oil until tender.
4) Add the vegetables, dill stalks, ginger, water, stock cube and pepper. Mix well and bring to boil.
5) Cover and simmer for approximately 40 minutes or until vegetables are tender. (The cooking time will vary depending on the size of your vegetable pieces). Stir at regular intervals.
6) Remove the dill stalks and then puree the soup with coconut milk and dill leaves.
7) Return to heat and warm through, then serve.

Potato, Pea and Mint Soup

Serves 4

This is a creamy, refreshing soup that is very quick and easy to make.

1 onion, roughly chopped
1 tbsp. olive oil
4 cups water
2 cloves garlic, crushed
1 vegetable stock cube
800g potatoes, peeled and roughly chopped
freshly ground black pepper, to season
2 cups peas
1 cup mint leaves (loosely packed)

1) Using a large saucepan or soup pot, stir fry onions in olive oil until tender.
2) Add water, garlic and stock cube.
3) Add the potatoes and pepper to the pot and, simmer covered, over medium heat until the potatoes are tender (approximately 15 minutes).
4) Add peas and simmer for a further 3 minutes.
5) Puree the soup with the mint in a food processor.
6) When done, return to the pot and reheat before serving.

Corn Chowder

Serves 4-5

This is a thick, creamy soup full of the flavour of corn and vegetables, perfect for a cold night.

5 medium-sized potatoes (approx. 750g)
1 onion, peeled and cut into quarters
1 tbsp. olive oil
4 large cloves garlic, crushed
5 cups water
1 vegetable stock cube
2 bay leaves
1 tsp. dried thyme
6 cups corn kernels (this is just under 1kg frozen corn)
1 red capsicum, cut in half and seeded
1 large carrot, chopped into bite-sized pieces (approx. 180g)
1 stick celery, chopped into bite-sized pieces
½ cup fresh finely chopped coriander
1 cup milk
freshly ground black pepper, to season

1) Peel and roughly chop potatoes, then steam until tender.
2) Meanwhile, using a large saucepan or soup pot, stir fry the onion in olive oil until tender.
3) Add the garlic, water, stock cube, bay leaves, thyme and three quarters of the corn. Simmer until potatoes are done. When potatoes are done add to the pot and simmer soup for a further 15 minutes.
4) Puree the soup in a food processor or blender and then return to the pot.
5) Add capsicum, carrot, celery and remaining corn. Simmer for 10 minutes, stirring often.
6) Right before serving, stir in the coriander and milk and season with pepper.

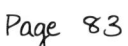

Minestrone Soup

Serves 4-5

This is a traditional Italian soup, which is a meal in itself, complete with vegetables, beans and pasta.

½ cup dried canellini beans (1¼ cups cooked)
1 onion, finely chopped
1 tbsp. olive oil
3 large cloves garlic, crushed
6 medium-sized tomatoes, diced (approx. 900g)
2 tbsp. tomato paste
2 cups water
1 vegetable stock cube
1 tsp. mixed herbs
2 bay leaves
1 large carrot, cut into small pieces (approx. 180g)
1 stick celery, cut into small pieces
½ tsp. freshly ground black pepper
1½ cups dry macaroni or other small pasta
¼ cup fresh finely chopped parsley

1) If you are using dried canellini beans, prepare them according to directions on page 18.
2) Meanwhile, using a large saucepan or soup pot, stir fry onion in olive oil until tender.
3) Add the garlic, tomatoes, tomato paste, water, stock cube, mixed herbs and bay leaves. Simmer for 5 minutes.
4) Add the beans, carrot, celery and pepper and simmer for 15 minutes, stirring often.
5) Meanwhile, cook the macaroni in boiling water until tender. Drain and rinse.
6) Before serving, stir in the macaroni and parsley, then remove the bay leaves and serve.

Turkish Bean Soup

Serves 4-5

This is a traditional Turkish soup, based on beans and tomatoes with a hint of lemon and cinnamon.

1 cup dried canellini beans (2½ cups cooked)
1 onion, finely chopped
1 tbsp. olive oil
½ tsp. ground cinnamon
1 tsp. ground paprika
6 medium-sized tomatoes, diced (approx. 900g)
4 large cloves garlic, crushed
½ tsp. freshly ground black pepper
3 cups water
1 tsp. dried oregano
juice from ½ large lemon
1 tsp. unrefined sugar
1 large carrot, cut into small pieces (approx. 180g)
1½ cups chopped green beans
¼ cup finely chopped parsley
¼ tsp. sea salt

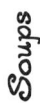

1) If you are using dried canellini beans, prepare them according to directions on page 18.
2) In a large saucepan, stir fry onion in olive oil until tender.
3) Remove from heat and add the cinnamon and paprika. Return to heat and stir for one minute.
4) Add the tomatoes, garlic and pepper, and simmer, covered for 5 minutes, stirring occasionally. The tomatoes should be quite mushy by this time.
5) Add the water, oregano, lemon juice, sugar and cooked beans. Stir, then simmer, covered for 10 minutes.
6) Add the carrot and green beans. Simmer for a further 10 minutes.
7) Stir in the parsley and salt then serve.

Tofu & Vegetables

"But for the sake of some little mouthful of flesh, we deprive a soul of the sun and light and of that proportion of life and time it had been born into the world to enjoy."
Plutarch

Main Dishes - Tofu & Vegetables

Tofu & Vegetables

"You are what you eat."

Shanta's Nifty Tofu Tip

The texture of tofu can vary from silky smooth to spongy or meaty. I am not a big fan of the spongelike texture of firm tofu and tended to avoid it until my aunty, Shanta taught me a great technique for changing that texture.

Steps to make your tofu less spongy and more meaty

1) Take a block of firm tofu (still in its packaging) and freeze.
2) Remove from freezer and defrost.
3) Remove from packaging and squeeze as much of the water as possible from the block.
4) Proceed with the recipe.

Tofu & Vegetables

Tofu on ice

Saucy Garlic Potatoes with Dill

Serves 2-3

This is a simple dish combining potatoes and chickpeas in a thick sauce with the flavours of dill, garlic and tomato. Serve with rice.

creative tip: Try using other vegetables instead of just potatoes.

½ cup dried chickpeas (1¼ cups cooked)
3 medium-sized potatoes, (approx. 450g)
2 spring onions, finely chopped
1 tbsp. olive oil
5 cloves garlic, crushed
1 small red chilli, seeded and finely chopped.
1 tsp. ground cumin
2 cups water
4 tbsp. tomato paste
½ cup chopped fresh dill
pinch of sea salt

1) If you are using dried chickpeas, prepare them according to directions on page 19.
2) Peel potatoes, cut into chunks and steam until just tender.
3) In a medium-sized saucepan, stir fry spring onions in olive oil until tender.
4) Remove from heat and add garlic, chilli and cumin.
5) Return to heat and stir fry for one minute and then add potatoes. Stir to coat.
6) Add water, tomato paste, chickpeas and potatoes and bring to the boil.
7) Simmer for 20 minutes, stirring often.
8) Add the dill and salt just before serving and mix well.

Tofu & Vegetables

Moroccan Vegetables with Couscous

Serves 4-5

This dish combines the delicate flavours of dill and cinnamon with a mixture of root vegetables and chickpeas.

½ cup dried chickpeas (1¼ cups cooked)
1 medium-sized onion, chopped
1 tbsp. olive oil
3 cloves garlic, crushed
1 tsp. turmeric
1 tsp. curry powder
1 tsp. ground cinnamon
1 tbsp. fresh grated ginger
1 capsicum, chopped
2 cups water
6 tbsp. tomato paste
1 vegetable stock cube
1 large carrot, cut into strips (approx. 180g)
300g swede, peeled and cut into strips
200g peeled sweet potato, cut into strips
2 cups couscous
2 cups water
2 tbsp. vegan margarine
1 small zucchini, cut into strips (approx. 150g)
5 tbsp. fresh chopped dill

1) If you are using dried chickpeas, prepare them according to directions on page 19.
2) Using a large saucepan or soup pot, stir fry the onion in olive oil until tender, then lower heat and add garlic, turmeric, curry powder, cinnamon and ginger, being careful not to burn. Stir fry for 30 seconds.
3) Add capsicum, water, tomato paste, stock cube and chickpeas and bring to the boil.

4) Add carrot, swede and sweet potato, and simmer over medium heat for 10-12 minutes or until vegetables are just tender. The time will vary depending on the size of your vegetable pieces.
6) Meanwhile, prepare the couscous according to directions on page 23.
7) Add zucchini and dill, and simmer on low heat for a further 3 minutes. Stir regularly during this time.
8) Serve the vegetables over the top of the couscous.

Dilled Spinach with Mushrooms

Serves 4

This is a simple light meal, full of natural flavour. Make sure you don't boil or overcook the spinach. Only ever cook it on your lowest heat setting.

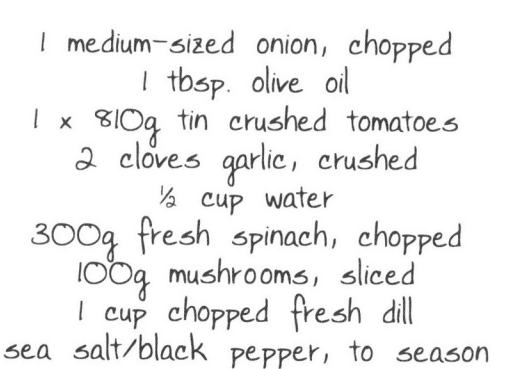

1 medium-sized onion, chopped
1 tbsp. olive oil
1 x 810g tin crushed tomatoes
2 cloves garlic, crushed
½ cup water
300g fresh spinach, chopped
100g mushrooms, sliced
1 cup chopped fresh dill
sea salt/black pepper, to season

1) In a medium-sized saucepan, stir fry onion in olive oil until tender.
2) Add tomatoes and garlic and bring to the boil.
3) Simmer for 10 minutes on low heat.
4) Add water, spinach, mushrooms, dill and salt/pepper and mix well.
5) Cover and simmer on low heat for 5 minutes. Add more water if necessary.
6) Serve over brown rice.

Mixed Vegetable & Apricot Curry

Serves 4

This meal is a mixture of Indian spices and fresh vegetables. Serve over boiled rice.

7 cups chopped mixed vegetables*
1 onion, roughly chopped
3cm piece fresh peeled ginger
2 large cloves garlic
1 small red chilli, seeded and chopped
3 bay leaves
2 tbsp. olive oil
1 tsp. garam masala
1 tsp. turmeric
1 tsp. ground coriander
2 medium-sized tomatoes (approx. 300g), diced
1 cup water
handful of dried apricots, (approx. 15 small sized), finely chopped
sea salt to season
5 tbsp. soy milk
¼ cup fresh chopped coriander

*Use whatever vegetables you prefer.

1) If you are using potato or sweet potato, steam until just tender, then set aside.
2) Puree the onion, ginger, garlic and chilli until it forms a paste.
3) In a large saucepan, fry the bay leaves in olive oil until they change colour.
4) Add the onion paste and stir fry for 1 minute.
5) Remove from heat and add the spices. Return to heat and stir for 30 seconds.
6) Add the tomatoes, water, apricots and salt. Simmer covered for 5 minutes, then add the harder vegetables (e.g. carrots, pumpkin)
7) Simmer, stirring occasionally until vegetables are tender and then add the softer vegetables (e.g. steamed potatoes, zucchini, mushrooms, broccoli).
8) When all vegetables are cooked, stir in the soy milk and coriander before serving.

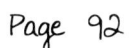

Tofu & Vegetables

Pumpkin & Sweet Potato Masala

Serves 4

This is a very sweet, creamy curry with a blend of Indian spices and chilli.

1 tbsp. olive oil
1 medium-sized onion, chopped
5 cloves garlic, crushed
1 small chilli, seeded and finely chopped
1 tsp. ground cumin
1 tsp. ground coriander
1 tsp. garam masala
600g peeled pumpkin, diced
600g peeled sweet potato, diced
2 tbsp. tamari sauce
2 tbsp. water
1 tsp. dried tarragon
270ml coconut cream/milk
1 cup fresh chopped coriander

1) In a large saucepan, stir fry onion in olive oil until tender.
2) Remove from heat and add garlic, chilli and spices.
3) Return to heat and fry for one minute, stirring constantly.
4) Add pumpkin, sweet potato, tamari sauce and water. Stir well and cover for 5 minutes.
5) Add coconut cream/milk and tarragon. Simmer with lid on, stirring often, until the pumpkin and sweet potato are soft. This should take 10-15 minutes, depending on the size of the vegetable pieces.
6) Once the pumpkin and sweet potato are ready, remove saucepan from heat and stir in the coriander.

Vegetables and Tofu in Sweet Tamari Marinade

Serves 4

A mixture of vegetables and tofu in a delicately sweet, Asian-style sauce.

1 tbsp. fresh grated ginger
3 cloves garlic, crushed
2 tbsp. tamari sauce
2 tbsp. rice syrup
1 tsp. dried rosemary
6 fresh lime leaves, chopped
½ cup boiling water
285g firm tofu, diced
1 medium-sized onion, chopped
1 tbsp. mustard seeds
1 tbsp. sesame oil
1 large carrot, chopped (approx. 180g)
1 capsicum, diced
1 cup sliced mushrooms
1 cup chopped broccoli
1 medium-sized zucchini, chopped (approx. 250g)

1) Combine ginger, garlic, tamari sauce, rice syrup, rosemary, lime leaves and boiling water in a deep dish.
2) Stir until rice syrup is completely dissolved and marinade is mixed well.
3) Add the tofu to the marinade and mix so that all pieces are well coated. Cover and refrigerate for at least 1 hour.
4) In a wok or large frying pan, stir fry onion and mustard seeds in olive oil until onion is tender.
5) Drain the tofu (keeping the marinade to one side) and add it to the pan. Stir fry until it starts to brown.
6) Add the carrots and keep stirring so that nothing sticks to the bottom of the pan.
7) After 5 minutes add the remaining vegetables and marinade, and simmer gently for a couple of minutes, making sure the vegetables stay crisp.
8) Serve over boiled rice or noodles.

Mushroom Steaks

Serves 4

These steaks are a perfect accompaniment to roast vegetables and Cashew & Pepper Gravy (page 142)

250g Portobello mushrooms
1 onion, grated
2 cloves garlic, crushed
½ cup finely chopped parsley
½ tsp. crushed black peppercorns
pinch of sea salt
1 tbsp. tamari sauce
1 cup breadcrumbs
vegetable oil for frying

1) Puree the mushrooms in a blender, then place into a mixing bowl.
2) Add onion, garlic, parsley, peppercorns, salt and tamari sauce. Mix until well combined.
3) Add the breadcrumbs and mix until evenly distributed.
4) Form the mixture into patties then pan fry them in olive oil until brown on both sides. Keep the heat on medium/low so that they do not cook too quickly. Serve immediately.

Lemon & Thyme Roast

Serves 4

An arrangement of roast vegetables and tofu in a lemon, garlic and thyme marinade.

2 tsp. black peppercorns
1 bunch of thyme (½ tightly packed cup)
3 cloves garlic, crushed
4 tbsp. olive oil
1 tbsp. tamari sauce
juice of 2 large lemons
250g firm tofu, cut into 1cm thick strips
800g potatoes, scrubbed and roughly chopped
800g sweet potatoes, peeled and roughly chopped

1) Crush peppercorns in a mortar and pestle, then pour into a small mixing bowl.
2) Roughly chop the thyme and then place into the mortar and pestle.
3) Pound the thyme until the woody stalks become soft, then add to the mixing bowl.
4) Add the garlic, olive oil, tamari sauce and lemon juice to the bowl and mix well.
5) In a very large baking tray, lay out the tofu and vegetables.
6) Pour the marinade evenly over the contents of the baking tray, making sure you evenly distribute the thyme.
7) Leave for 1-2 hours (the longer the better). Throughout this time, it is a good idea to tip the baking tray every now and then so that the liquid runs to one corner, and spoon it over the vegetables and tofu.
8) Pre-heat the oven to 180°C. Before baking, remove tofu from the dish. Bake for 45-60 minutes (depending on the size of your vegetable pieces.) Add the tofu once the vegetables just start to become tender, as it will only need about 30 minutes.
9) Serve with your choice of greens.

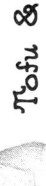

Bombay Potatoes

Serves 4

This is a classic Indian dish that is full of flavour. I like to serve it with pappadums.

> 6 medium-sized potatoes, scrubbed (approx. 900g)
> 1 onion, chopped
> 1 tbsp. olive oil
> 3 cloves garlic, crushed
> 1 tbsp. fresh grated ginger
> 2 tsp. cumin seeds
> 2 tsp. mustard seeds
> 1 tsp. turmeric
> 1 tsp. ground paprika
> 1 tsp. ground coriander
> ½ tsp. ground fenugreek
> ½ tsp. mixed spice
> ½ tsp. sea salt
> 1 x 415g tin chopped tomatoes
> 1 tbsp. unrefined brown sugar
> ½ cup fresh chopped coriander
> freshly ground black pepper, to season

1) Chop potatoes into bite size pieces and steam until just tender (10-15 minutes).
2) In a large saucepan, stir fry the onion in olive oil until tender.
3) Remove from heat and add garlic, ginger, cumin seeds and mustard seeds. Return to heat and stir for one minute.
4) Add the remaining spices, and stir for another 30 seconds.
5) Add potatoes and stir until well coated.
6) Add the salt, tomatoes and brown sugar. Leave to simmer for 10 minutes. By adding the sugar, you will neutralise the acidity of the tomatoes and bring out a richer flavour.
7) Add the coriander, and season with pepper just before serving.
8) Serve with rice or as a vegetable side dish.

Vegetable and Tofu Stroganoff

Serves 4

This is an adaptation of traditional beef stroganoff and I find it works well with any vegetables and/or tofu. Don't be limited by the ones I have chosen. This recipe is best served over boiled rice or rice noodles.

1 large carrot (approx. 180g)
400g peeled sweet potato
1 small zucchini (approx. 150g)
200g mushrooms
150g green beans
1 tbsp. vegan margarine
1 onion, chopped
1 tbsp. mustard seeds
2 cloves garlic, crushed
2 cups water
1 vegetable stock cube
1 tbsp. tamari sauce
Freshly ground black pepper, to season
3 tbsp. tomato paste
150g firm tofu, diced
1 tbsp. vegan margarine, extra
1 tbsp. arrowroot
6 tbsp. soy yoghurt
2 tbsp. fresh chopped parsley

1) Chop vegetables into bite size pieces (keeping separate vegetables divided), and leave to one side.
2) In a large saucepan, melt the margarine and then add the onion. Stir fry until tender.
3) Add the mustard seeds and garlic, and stir for 1 minute.
4) Add the sweet potato and toss through the onion mixture for a few minutes, adding a little of the water every now and then to moisten the pan.

5) Once the sweet potato starts to darken in colour, add the rest of the water, stock cube, tamari sauce, pepper, tomato paste and tofu.
6) Add the carrot and simmer for 5-10 minutes. The sweet potato should be soft by this time.
7) In the meantime, stir fry the mushrooms in a small saucepan in extra margarine. Cook for about 6-7 minutes.
8) Add mushrooms, zucchini and beans to the sauce and simmer for a further 5 minutes.
9) Mix the arrowroot with just enough water to make a thick liquid and add to the stroganoff. Make sure you stir constantly while you add the arrowroot, as it will cause the sauce to thicken.
10) Just before serving, stir in the soy yoghurt and parsley.

Tofu & Vegetables

Eggplant Wraps with Minted Couscous

Serves 4

You could call this a Middle Eastern-style burrito. With the fragrant flavours of cinnamon, mint and parsley. This dish is best served with a green salad.

1 large eggplant, peeled and cut into strips
1 onion, finely chopped
1 tbsp. olive oil
2 cloves garlic, crushed
1 tsp. ground paprika
3 medium-sized tomatoes, diced (approx. 450g)
1 red capsicum, diced
1 tsp. dried oregano
½ tsp. ground cinnamon
2 tbsp. tomato paste
2 tbsp. fresh finely chopped flat leaf parsley
1 tbsp. fresh finely chopped mint leaves
4-5 large flour tortillas
2 cups couscous
2 cups water
2 tbsp. vegan margarine
1 tbsp. fresh finely chopped flat leaf parsley, extra
juice of ½ lemon
sea salt/black pepper, to season

1) Bleed the eggplant according to directions on page 25.
2) In a medium-sized saucepan, stir fry the onion in olive oil until tender.
3) Add the garlic and paprika, and stir fry for a minute.
4) Add the eggplant, tomatoes, capsicum, oregano, cinnamon and tomato paste.
5) Mix well and simmer with the lid on for 20 minutes, stirring occasionally. After 20 minutes, all vegetables should be soft.
6) Pre-heat the oven to 180°C.
7) Stir the parsley and mint in to the eggplant mixture.

8) Spoon eggplant mixture across the first tortilla about third of the way in and then roll, ending with the final edge turned to the bottom. Repeat with remaining tortillas.
9) Place onto a baking tray and bake in the oven for 10 minutes (they should be just browned).
10) Meanwhile, prepare couscous according to directions on page 23.
11) Combine the extra parsley, lemon juice, salt and pepper, then pour over the couscous. Fluff with a fork until well combined and couscous is without lumps.
12) Serve the wraps on a bed of couscous and accompany with your favourite salad.

Tofu & Vegetables

Beans & Pulses

"I cannot fish without falling a little in self-respect...always when I have done I feel it would have been better if I had not fished."
Henry David Thoreau

Main Dishes - Beans and Pulses

Beans & Pulses

Indian Dahl

Serves 4

This recipe is quick, easy and very tasty. It combines nutritious lentils with Indian spices to form a hearty meal. Dahl can be adapted in countless ways. I have provided only two dahl recipes: Indian Dahl and Two Lentil Dahl, but don't let that limit you. There are a variety of herbs and spices that may be added in different quantities to produce many different flavours.

2 cups red lentils
1 tbsp. olive oil
1 medium-sized onion, chopped
4 cloves garlic, crushed
2 tbsp. fresh grated ginger
2 tsp. fennel seeds
2 tsp. turmeric
1 tbsp. garam masala
2 tsp. ground paprika
1 tbsp. ground cumin
5 cups water
1 vegetable stock cube
1 cup fresh chopped coriander

1) Rinse lentils until the water runs clear and set aside.
2) In a medium-sized saucepan, fry onion in olive oil until tender.
3) Add garlic, ginger and spices, and stir quickly over medium heat for one minute.
4) Add lentils with water and stock cube and bring to the boil.
5) Simmer over medium heat for approximately 15 minutes, stirring often to ensure lentils do not stick to the bottom of the pan.
6) Once lentils have formed a puree-like texture, stir in the coriander and serve over boiled rice with pappadums (optional).

Beans & Pulses

Two Lentil Dahl

Serves 4

This Dahl has a tomato flavour and adds another colour with the green lentils that does wonders for presentation. This is probably a better choice if you are to have guests or if you would like to try something different to the original Dahl recipe.

1 cup dried green lentils (3 cups cooked)
1 cup red lentils
1 medium-sized onion, chopped
1 tbsp. olive oil
4 cloves garlic, crushed
2 tbsp. fresh grated ginger
1 tbsp. black onion seeds (optional)
2 tsp. fennel seeds
2 tsp. garam masala
½ tbsp. turmeric
2 tsp. ground paprika
1 tbsp. ground cumin
2 cups water
1 tbsp. tamarind paste
1 x 415g tin crushed tomatoes
¾ cup fresh chopped coriander
½ tsp. sea salt

1) Prepare green lentils according to directions on page 21.
2) Rinse red lentils until the water runs clear and set aside.
3) In a medium-sized saucepan, fry onion in olive oil until tender.
4) Remove from heat and add garlic, ginger, black onion seeds, fennel seeds and spices.
5) Return to medium heat and stir quickly for 1 minute. This will release the flavour of the spices.
6) Add water, tamarind, crushed tomatoes and red lentils. Stir well.
7) Simmer over medium heat for approximately 15 minutes, stirring often to ensure lentils do not stick to the bottom of the pan.
8) Once red lentils start to soften, add green lentils to the pot. Mix well and simmer for a further 5 minutes, stirring often.
9) Before serving, stir in the coriander and salt. Serve over boiled rice with pappadums (optional).

Chilli Con Carne

Serves 4

Don't be shocked by the addition of a small amount of cocoa to this dish. It actually improves the colour and taste, making it richer. Chilli Con Carne is great served with grilled slices of Polenta, warm bread or boiled rice.

Creative tip: Use this dish as a filling for home made pies or pastry parcels

1 cup dried red kidney beans (3 cups cooked)
1 red onion, chopped
1 tbsp. olive oil
1 large red chilli, seeded and finely chopped
3 cloves garlic, crushed
1 tbsp. ground cumin
1 tbsp. ground paprika
1 x 415g tin crushed tomatoes
4 tbsp. tomato paste
1 cup water
1 tbsp. cocoa
2 tsp. mixed herbs
1 cup textured vegetable protein (TVP)
½ tsp. sea salt
1 cup fresh chopped parsley (optional)

1) If you are using dried kidney beans, prepare them according to directions on page 17.
2) In a medium-sized saucepan, fry onion in oil until tender.
3) Add chilli, garlic, cumin and paprika and stir for 1 minute.
4) Add tinned tomatoes, tomato paste, water, cocoa, and mixed herbs, and simmer for 5 minutes, stirring often.
5) Add the beans and TVP. The mixture should now start to thicken as the TVP absorbs the excess liquid.
6) Allow to simmer for 20 minutes, stirring often.
7) Right before serving, stir in the salt and parsley.

Gentle Lentil Stew

Serves 4-5

This meal is easy to prepare and very wholesome. It can be modified according to the vegetables you have available. Also, try varying the herbs you use for different flavours.

1 cup red lentils
1 medium-sized onion, chopped
1 tbsp. olive oil
1 capsicum, finely chopped
3 large cloves garlic, crushed
4 medium-sized tomatoes, diced (approx. 600g)
1 x 415g tin crushed tomatoes
2 tbsp. tamari sauce
1 cup water
3 tbsp. tomato paste
freshly ground black pepper, to season
1 large carrot, chopped (approx. 180g)
1 small zucchini, sliced (approx. 150g)
1 very full cup broccoli florets
½ cup fresh chopped basil leaves

1) Rinse lentils until the water runs clear and set aside.
2) In a medium-sized saucepan, stir fry onion in olive oil until tender.
3) Add capsicum and stir until it starts to soften.
4) Add garlic and fresh tomatoes and simmer for 5 minutes with the lid on.
5) Add crushed tomatoes, tamari sauce, water, tomato paste and lentils.
6) Simmer for approximately 20 minutes, stirring often.
7) Add pepper and carrot, and simmer for a further 10 minutes.
8) Add zucchini, broccoli and basil, and mix well. Leave to stand with lid on for 5 minutes.
9) Serve on its own or over boiled rice.

Vegetable Dhansak

Serves 4

Dhansak is an Indian dish that combines lentils and chickpeas with vegetables. The sauce has a sweet and sour taste owing to the pineapple, lemon juice and spices. The addition of chilli is optional because it tastes good with or without.

½ cup dried chickpeas (1¼ cups cooked)
¾ cup red lentils
1 tbsp. olive oil
1 onion, chopped
3 large cloves garlic, crushed
1 small red chilli, seeded and finely chopped (optional)
2 tbsp. fresh grated ginger
1 tbsp. cumin seeds
1 tsp. garam masala
2 tsp. ground paprika
1 tsp. curry powder
3 medium-sized tomatoes, diced (approx. 450g)
1 capsicum, diced
½ cup crushed pineapple (fresh or unsweetened tinned)
4 tbsp. tomato paste
1 ¼ cups water
1 large carrot, chopped into small pieces (approx. 180g)
sea salt, to season
juice of ½ lemon
1 cup chopped green beans
1 cup sliced mushrooms
½ cup fresh chopped coriander

1) If you are using dried chickpeas, prepare them according to directions on page 19.
2) Rinse lentils until the water runs clear and set aside.
3) In a large saucepan, stir fry the onion in olive oil until tender.
4) Remove from heat and add the garlic, chilli, ginger and spices, then return to heat and stir for 1 minute.

5) Add the tomatoes, capsicum, pineapple, tomato paste, water, lentils and chickpeas. Mix well.
6) Simmer with the lid on until the lentils are soft (about 20 minutes). Stir often to make sure the lentils don't stick to the pan.
7) Add the carrot, and season with salt. Simmer, covered for a further 5 minutes.
8) Add the lemon juice, beans and mushrooms, and remove from the heat. Leave to stand with the lid on for 10 minutes and then stir in the coriander before serving.

"you didn't fill my bowl!"

Golden Masala

Serves 4

This dish is a combination of aromatic spices, split peas and spinach. It is best served with basmati rice.

1½ cups yellow split peas
1 tbsp. olive oil
1 onion, finely chopped
1 tsp. garam masala
2 tsp. ground coriander
1 tsp. ground cumin
3 cloves garlic, crushed
1½ tbsp. fresh grated ginger
3 medium-sized tomatoes, chopped (approx. 450g)
½ cup grated apple
3 tbsp. tomato paste
½ cup water
sea salt, to season
2 tightly packed cups chopped spinach

1) Cook split peas according to directions on page 21.
2) In a medium-sized saucepan, stir fry the onion in the olive oil until tender.
3) Remove from heat and add spices, garlic and ginger, and then return to heat and stir for one minute.
4) Add the tomatoes, apple, tomato paste and water, and simmer covered until tomatoes are soft and mushy.
5) Stir split peas into tomato mixture and then season with salt and pepper. Leave to simmer a further 15 minutes with the lid on. Stir occasionally.
6) Season to taste with salt and then remove from heat and stir in the spinach before serving. You will find the heat from the saucepan will cook the spinach.

Bean and Spinach Stew

Serves 4

This is a tasty versatile stew. You can keep the peppery tomato sauce and compliment it with beans or vegies of your choice.

½ cup dried kidney beans (1½ cups cooked)
½ cup dried blackeye beans (1½ cups cooked)
1 onion, chopped
1 tbsp. olive oil
3 cloves garlic, crushed
2 tsp. mustard seeds
2 tsp. fennel seeds
1 x 415g tin crushed tomatoes
1 tbsp. miso
1 tbsp. tamari sauce
½ cup water
½ tsp. black peppercorns
2 sprigs rosemary leaves
3 tightly packed cups finely chopped spinach

1) If you are using dried kidney or blackeye beans, prepare them according to directions on page 17.
2) In a medium-sized saucepan, stir fry the onion in olive oil until tender.
3) Add the garlic, mustard seeds and fennel seeds, and stir for one minute.
4) Add the tomatoes, miso, tamari sauce and water, and mix well. Leave to simmer with lid on for a few minutes.
5) Meanwhile, crush the peppercorns roughly with a mortar and pestle, and then add to the saucepan with the beans.
6) Simmer with the lid on, stirring occasionally for 20 minutes.
7) Add the rosemary and simmer for a further 5 minutes.
8) Stir in the spinach and simmer until it shrinks (a few minutes).
9) Serve with rice.

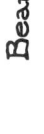

Lentil and Bean Stew

Serves 4-5

This hearty stew goes well with brown rice or millet and a green salad.

½ cup dried pinto or borlotti beans (1½ cups cooked)
1 cup red lentils
1 onion, chopped
1 tbsp. olive oil
3 cloves garlic, crushed
1 tbsp. fresh grated ginger
1 tbsp. yellow mustard seeds
1 kg tomatoes, cubed
½ cup water
2 tbsp. tomato paste
1 tbsp. blackstrap molasses
3 tbsp. tamari sauce
1 large carrot, chopped (approx. 180g)
2 sticks celery, chopped
½ cup fresh finely chopped parsley

Beans & Pulses

1) If you are using dried beans, prepare them according to directions on page 16.
2) Rinse lentils until the water runs clear and set aside.
3) In a medium-sized saucepan, stir fry the onion in olive oil until tender.
4) Remove from heat and add the garlic, ginger and mustard seeds. Return to heat and stir for one minute.
5) Add the tomatoes, water, tomato paste, molasses and tamari sauce. Leave to simmer with lid on for a few minutes until the tomatoes go mushy.
6) Add the beans and lentils and simmer with the lid on for 10 minutes, stirring occasionally.
7) Add the carrot and celery and simmer for a further 15 minutes.
8) Just before serving, stir in the parsley.

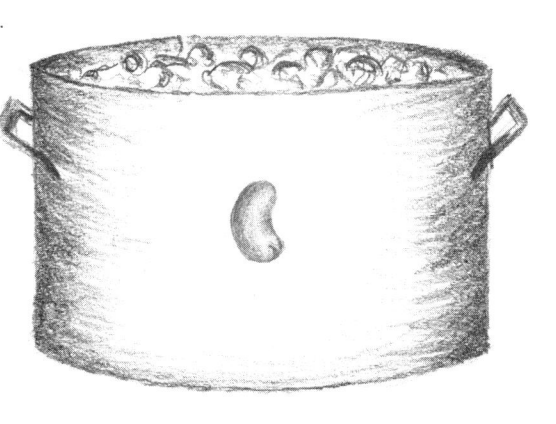

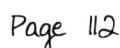

Potato and Lentil Bake

Serves 5-6

This dish is a tasty alternative to the usual, creamy potato bake.

1 cup red lentils
1 tbsp. olive oil
1 medium-sized onion, chopped
4 cloves garlic, crushed
1 tbsp. ground cumin
1 cup water
1 vegetable stock cube
1 x 810g tin crushed tomatoes
1 tbsp. mixed herbs
2 tbsp. tamari sauce
450g sweet potatoes
3 medium-sized potatoes (approx. 450g)
2 medium-sized carrots, chopped (approx. 200g)
4 sticks celery, chopped
1-2 tbsp. vegan margarine
1 tbsp. dried mixed herbs, extra
grated soy cheese to top (optional)

1) Rinse lentils until the water runs clear and set aside.
2) In a large saucepan, fry onion in olive oil until tender.
3) Add garlic and cumin, and stir fry for one minute.
4) Add lentils, water, stock cube, tomatoes, herbs and tamari sauce. Mix well.
5) Simmer over medium heat until lentils become soft, stirring often to make sure lentils do not stick to the bottom of the pan.
6) Meanwhile, pre-heat oven to 180°C.
7) Peel sweet potato and scrub potatoes, and then slice thinly.
8) Once lentils are cooked, remove from heat, and add carrots and celery.
9) Layer a 30cm x 19cm baking dish with sliced potato.
10) Add a layer of lentil mixture.
11) Next, layer the sweet potato and keep layering the lentil mixture and potatoes until both have run out. The last layer will be a mixture of normal and sweet potato.
12) Spread the top layer of potato with vegan margarine and mixed herbs or as an alternative, top with soy cheese and herbs.
13) Bake in the oven for 45-60 minutes (until potato is soft).

Moroccan Chickpea Casserole

Serves 4

Casseroles are very easy because there is so little work involved. This one uses Moroccan spices and tomatoes and goes extremely well with couscous (included in the ingredients). If you don't have couscous, serve with rice.

1 ½ cups chickpeas (3¾ cups cooked)
1 medium-sized onion, chopped
3 large cloves garlic, crushed
1 red or yellow capsicum, chopped
3 medium-sized tomatoes, diced (approx. 450g)
1 small green chilli, seeded and finely chopped
juice of ½ lemon
2 tbsp. sweet paprika
1 tsp. ground cumin
2 tsp. fennel seeds
1 tsp. turmeric
2 tbsp. tomato paste
½ tsp. sea salt
1 cinnamon stick
2 cups couscous
2 cups boiling water
2 tbsp. vegan margarine
1 firmly packed tbsp. fresh finely chopped coriander
1 firmly packed tbsp. fresh finely chopped parsley
1 firmly packed tbsp. fresh finely chopped mint

1) If you are using dried chickpeas, prepare them according to the directions on page 19.
2) Pre-heat the oven to 170°C.
3) Place all ingredients down to and including the cinnamon stick, into a casserole dish and mix well.
4) Bake with the lid on for 1 hour, stirring every 15 minutes.
5) Just before the casserole is ready, prepare the couscous according to the directions on page 23.
6) Stir the herbs into the casserole and serve with the couscous.

Beans & Pulses

Lentil Loaf

Serves 4-5

Lentil loaf is a great accompaniment to roast vegetables and it replaces the meat in a meal. It is delicious served with Cashew and Pepper Gravy (page 142).

½ cup brown rice
1 cup red lentils
350g sweet potatoes, peeled and grated
1 medium-sized onion, grated
½ tsp. freshly ground black pepper
2 large cloves garlic, crushed
1 cup rolled oats
½ cup breadcrumbs
2 tbsp. savoury yeast flakes
¼ cup ground arrowroot
2 tbsp. tamari sauce
1 large sprig rosemary leaves (finely chopped)
2 tsp. cumin seeds
2 tsp. mustard seeds
½ tbsp. olive oil

1) Cook brown rice until tender. (For instructions see page 23)
2) Cook red lentils according to directions on page 20.
3) Meanwhile, pre-heat the oven to 180°C, then grease and line a 25cm x 13cm loaf tin.
4) In a large mixing bowl combine sweet potato, onion, pepper, garlic, rolled oats, breadcrumbs, yeast flakes, ground arrowroot, tamari sauce and rosemary.
5) In a small saucepan, fry the cumin and mustard seeds in the olive oil, then add to the bowl with the cooked rice and red lentils.
6) Mix all ingredients well, then press firmly into the loaf tin.
7) Bake for 35-40 minutes. Wait for 10 minutes before removing loaf from the tin. To remove, slide a knife around the edge and then turn onto a flat board or plate and peel the lining from the bottom.
8) Slice the loaf and serve.

Lentil and Barley Shepherd's Pie

Serves 4

This is an adaptation of the traditional pie made with minced meat. The lentils and barley provide a substantial substitute, and the added flavours of fresh herbs makes this a delicious and hearty meal.

creative tip: If you can find a decent soy cheese try sprinkling the top of the pie with the cheese before baking.

Beans & Pulses

1 cup dried green lentils (3 cups cooked)
1 cup pearl barley
1 medium-sized onion, chopped
1 tbsp. olive oil
1 x 415g tin crushed tomatoes
1 large carrot, diced (approx. 180g)
2 large cloves garlic, crushed
1 tsp. dried oregano
1 tsp. dried mixed herbs
3 tbsp. tomato paste
2 tbsp. tamari sauce
4 large sprigs fresh thyme
½ cup fresh chopped parsley
freshly ground black pepper, to season
pinch of sea salt

Topping
6 medium-sized potatoes (approx. 900g)
1 tbsp. vegan margarine
5 tbsp. soy milk
¼ cup fresh finely chopped parsley
freshly ground black pepper, to season

1) If you are using dried lentils, prepare them according to the directions on page 21. Prepare the barley the same way. (The lentils and barley may be cooked together).
2) Peel potatoes for the topping and roughly chop, then steam until tender.

3) Meanwhile, in a large saucepan, stir fry onion in olive oil until tender.
4) Add crushed tomatoes, carrot and garlic, and simmer for 5 minutes.
5) Add lentils, barley, oregano, mixed herbs, tamari sauce and tomato paste, and simmer for a further 5 minutes.
6) Pre-heat the oven to 180°C.
7) Remove mixture from heat and stir in the leaves from the thyme sprigs and the parsley. Season with pepper and salt.
8) Pour tomato mixture into a 21cm x 21cm baking dish and then pat it down flat.
9) Place potatoes, margarine, soy milk and pepper into a mixing bowl and mash until potatoes are smooth. For a creamier consistency, use an electric mixer – it is easier to spread over the top when prepared this way.
10) Add parsley and pepper and stir through.
11) Spread potato mixture over the lentil and barley mixture to about 2–3cm thick.
12) Bake for 25–30 minutes or until topping browns.

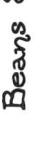

Burritos

Serves 4–5

Following are the main ingredients for a Mexican meal. You can then vary them as you wish (see my suggestions below the recipe). The main flavours in any Mexican dish are coriander and lime, which are prevalent in the salsa and guacamole recipes.

Bean Filling
1 ½ cups dried pinto beans (4½ cups cooked)
1 red onion, finely chopped
1 tbsp. olive oil
1 large green chilli, seeded and finely chopped
1 tbsp. ground cumin
1 tsp. ground paprika
3 cloves garlic, crushed
1 capsicum
1 tsp. dried oregano
1 x 415g tin crushed tomatoes
3 tbsp. tomato paste
1 cup fresh chopped coriander

Accompaniments
4–5 large flour tortillas
boiled rice
1 quantity of Refreshing Guacamole (page 150)
1 quantity of Tomato Salsa (page 148)
shredded lettuce
grated soy cheese (optional)

1) If you are using dried pinto beans, prepare them according to directions on page 16.
2) Prepare any accompaniments you intend to serve.
3) Using a medium-sized saucepan, stir fry onion in olive oil until tender, then remove from heat and add chilli, cumin and garlic.
4) Return to heat and stir fry for one minute.
5) Add remaining ingredients except beans and coriander. Leave to simmer while you mash or puree half the beans.
6) Add these with the whole beans to the tomato mixture and simmer for 15–20 minutes, stirring often.

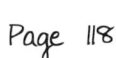

Beans & Pulses

7) Just before serving, add coriander and stir well.
8) Before serving the meal, heat tortillas in the oven or microwave until warm. (Do not warm too many in advance, as they will dry out once they cool down). If you are heating them in the oven, wrap them in foil to keep them moist.
9) To serve, place a strip of bean mixture and rice down the middle of the tortilla. Cover with any, or all of the fillings and roll the tortilla into a long parcel. Fold over at one end so that the filling does not fall out.

Other Uses for the same fillings

1) Nachos – Place beans and soy cheese over a bowl of corn chips. Grill and then serve with cold accompaniments.
2) Tacos – Layer the toppings inside warmed taco shells.
3) A Quesadilla style meal – (although Quesa means cheese in Mexican, you can take the same preparation idea and apply it to the different ingredients). To do this, place a flour tortilla in a lightly oiled frying pan and spoon rice, beans and soy cheese (optional) onto half of the tortilla, in a semicircle shape. Now fold the other half over so it resembles a folded pizza. Pan fry on both sides and serve topped with guacamole, salsa and lettuce.
4) Pan fry a tortilla on both sides and serve the toppings over the flat tortilla.
5) Or, just eat the beans, rice, guacamole and salsa as a meal.

Sample Burrito

Labels: Soft flour tortilla, Guacamole, Salsa, Shredded lettuce, Beany filling, Rice

Beans & Pulses

Boston Barbecue Beans

Serves 4

The barbecue sauce in this dish is rich and tasty, and the beans can be substituted with tofu or vegetables.

1 ½ cup dried navy or canellini beans (3¾ cups cooked)
5 medium-sized tomatoes, diced (approx. 750g)
1 tbsp. olive oil
1 medium-sized onion, chopped
3 large cloves garlic, crushed
½ cup apple juice
2 tbsp. tamari sauce
1 tsp. dried thyme
2 tsp. Dijon mustard
1 tbsp. apple cider vinegar
1 tbsp. tomato paste
1 tbsp. blackstrap molasses

1) If you are using dried beans, prepare according to directions on page 18.
2) In a medium-sized saucepan, stir fry the onion in olive oil until tender.
3) Add the remaining ingredients except the beans and mix well. Simmer for 5 minutes.
4) Add the beans and simmer for a further 15 minutes, stirring often.
5) Serve over brown rice.

Aduki Bean Stir Fry

Serves 4

A tasty noodle-based stir fry, which, because of the addition of the aduki beans and pinenuts, is quite filling.

1 cup dried aduki beans (3 cups cooked)
250g rice noodles
1 onion, finely chopped
1 tbsp. olive oil
1 small red chilli, seeded and finely chopped
3 cloves garlic, crushed
3 medium-sized tomatoes, chopped (approx. 450g)
2 tbsp. rice mirin
3 tbsp. tamari sauce
3 heaped cups stir fry vegetables*
100g pinenuts

* Stir fry vegetables may include carrots, mushrooms, baby corn, snowpeas, bean sprouts, broccoli and beans.

1) If you are using dried aduki beans, prepare them according to directions on page 18.
2) Cook rice noodles according to directions on the packet — they usually only take 3–5 minutes.
3) Drain the noodles, rinse the starch off and set aside.
4) In a wok or large frying pan, stir fry the onion in olive oil until tender.
5) Add the chilli and cook for 1 minute, stirring constantly.
6) Add the garlic, tomatoes, rice mirin and tamari sauce. Simmer until tomatoes are soft.
7) Add the aduki beans and any of the harder stir fry vegetables such as carrots or baby corn to the tomato mixture and return to medium heat to simmer for 5 minutes.
8) Add the remaining vegetables to the stir fry and mix through. Simmer until vegetables are tender then add the noodles. Mix well.
9) In a small saucepan, and without any oil, toss the pinenuts over medium heat until browned.
10) Just before serving, stir in the pinenuts.

Beans & Pulses

"The greatness of a nation can be judged by the way it's animals are treated."
Gandhi

Roice & Pasta

Main Dishes - Rice and Pasta

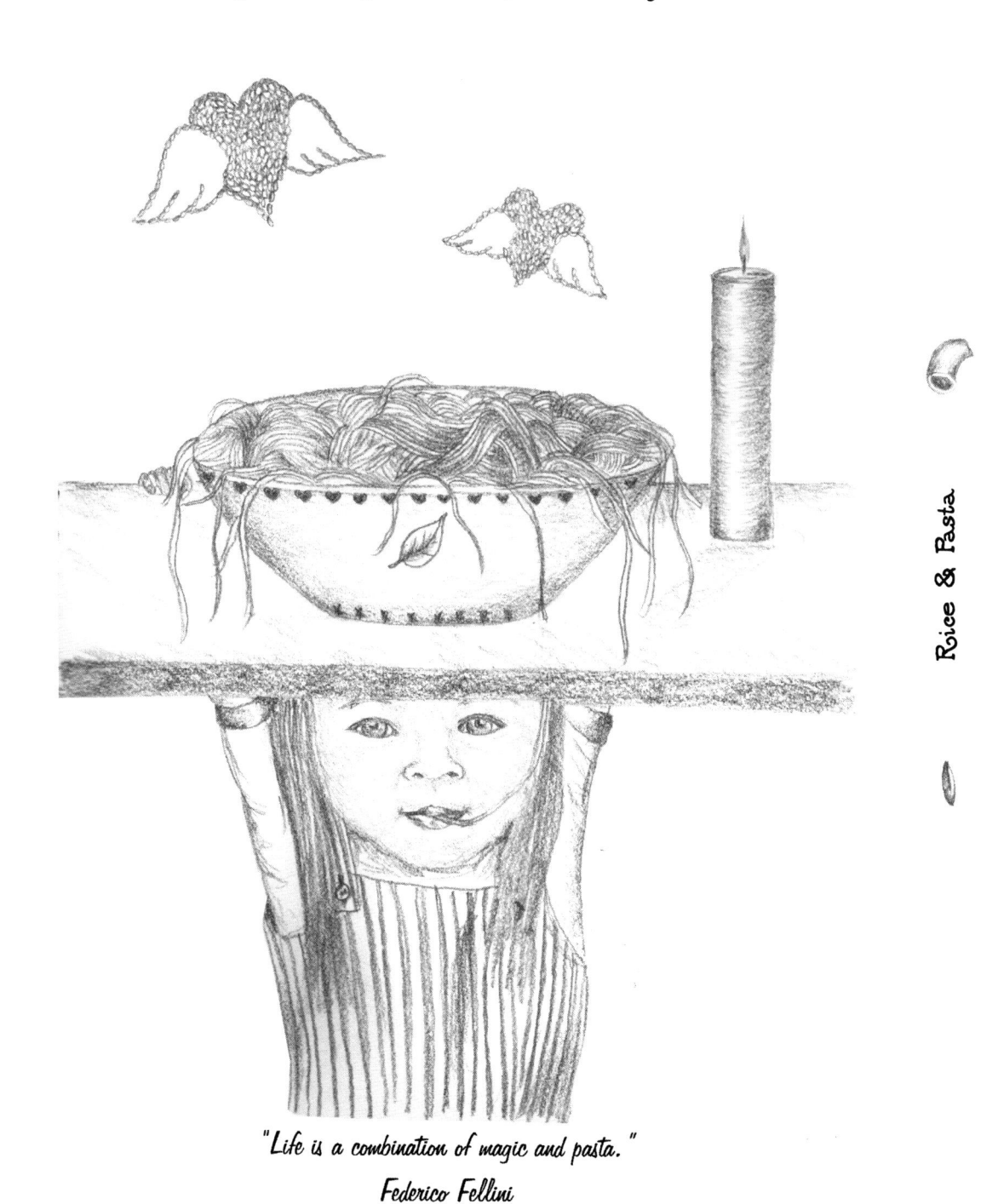

Rice & Pasta

"Life is a combination of magic and pasta."
Federico Fellini

Spaghetti Bolognese

Serves 4

This rich tomato sauce with lentils and fresh thyme provides a great, healthy alternative to traditional meaty spaghetti Bolognese.

creative tip — This dish can be used as a filling for homemade pies, is great as a stew with vegetables added or used as a sauce over baked vegetables.

1 cup red lentils
1 medium-sized onion, chopped
1 tbsp. olive oil
1 small chilli, seeded and finely chopped (optional)
3 cloves garlic, crushed
1 capsicum, finely chopped
1 x 415g tin crushed tomatoes
1 tsp. dried oregano
3 tbsp. tomato paste
2 tbsp. tamari sauce
1 cup water
300g spaghetti
¼ cup fresh chopped basil leaves

1) Rinse the lentils until the water runs clear, and set aside.
2) In a medium-sized saucepan, stir fry onion in olive oil until tender.
3) Add chilli, garlic and capsicum, and stir fry until capsicum is tender. Keep heat to a minimum, taking care not to burn the garlic.
4) Add crushed tomatoes, oregano, tomato paste, tamari sauce, water and lentils, and stir well over medium heat until sauce is simmering.
5) Cover and simmer for approximately 20 minutes or until lentils are soft. Stir the sauce occasionally, taking care not to let the lentils gather on the bottom of the pan.
6) Meanwhile, in a large saucepan, bring some water to the boil and add the spaghetti. Cook until tender stirring occasionally.
7) Before serving, stir the basil into the sauce and spoon over the spaghetti.

Henna's Sunflower and Bean Pasta

Serves 2-3

This sauce is quite different to traditional Italian sauces because of the contrasting flavours.

300g of your favourite pasta
½ cup sunflower seeds
1 x 420g tin four bean mix
2 cloves garlic, crushed
1 x 415g tin chopped tomatoes
2 tsp. lemon pepper
3 tbsp. vegan cream cheese

1) In a large saucepan, bring some water to the boil and add the pasta. Cook until tender.
2) Meanwhile, in a medium-sized saucepan, dry roast the sunflower seeds over medium heat.
3) Rinse beans and add with the garlic. Mix well.
4) Add tomatoes and lemon pepper and simmer for 5 minutes.
5) Add cream cheese and stir until mixture goes creamy.
6) Serve over the pasta.

Pesto & Tomato Spaghetti

Serves 4

The delicious tastes of basil and fresh tomatoes mark this dish. Not only is it tasty but very quick to prepare.

creative tip: Use the pesto ingredients as a dip, a pizza topping or as a spread on sandwiches with tomatoes and avocado. If you have a good soy cheese this will also compliment it well.

500g spaghetti
500g cherry tomatoes
3 large cloves garlic, crushed
½ tsp. sea salt
freshly ground black pepper, to season
100g pine nuts
100g fresh basil
3 tbsp. cold pressed olive oil

1) In a large saucepan, bring some water to the boil and add the spaghetti. Cook until tender.
2) Meanwhile, cut cherry tomatoes in half and place into a small saucepan with the garlic, sea salt and pepper. Simmer over low heat for 15 minutes.
3) In a food processor or blender, combine the pine nuts, basil and olive oil until it becomes a paste.
4) Once the spaghetti is ready, toss both the tomato mixture and the basil mixture through until all strands are evenly coated.
5) Serve warm or cool with a salad.

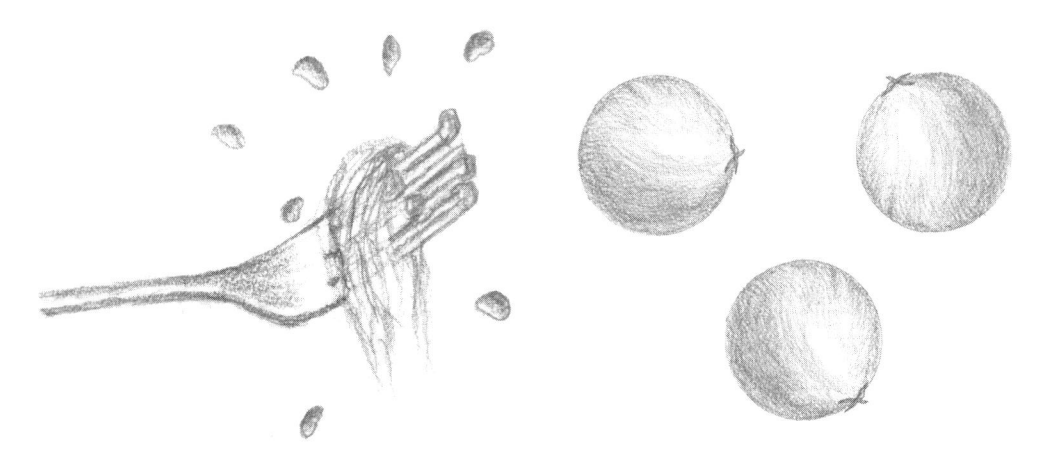

Herb Pasta with Sun-dried Tomatoes & Spinach

Serves 4

This dish can be served warm, or chilled as a salad. The fresh ingredients provide a mixture of refreshing flavours. I like to use either penne or spiral pasta for the visual affect.

375g of your favourite pasta
50g sun-dried tomatoes (not marinated)
100g pine nuts
250g cherry tomatoes
1 tbsp. olive oil
3 large cloves garlic, crushed
100g English spinach
2 tbsp. fresh finely chopped mint
2 tbsp. fresh finely chopped parsley
2 tbsp. fresh finely chopped basil

1) In a large saucepan, bring some water to the boil and add the pasta. Cook until tender.
2) Meanwhile, in a separate small saucepan, add sun-dried tomatoes to boiling water and cook for approximately 5 minutes. This will cause them to soften.
3) Dry-fry pine nuts until they start to brown, or, alternatively, lay the nuts out on a baking tray and bake at 180°C for 10 minutes. Once they are done, set aside.
4) Cut cherry tomatoes into halves.
5) Coarsely chop the sun-dried tomatoes.
6) Heat olive oil in a small saucepan, and add garlic and cherry tomatoes. Cover and cook until tender, being careful not to burn.
7) Add sun-dried tomatoes and simmer for a couple of minutes.
8) Remove from heat.
9) In a large bowl, stir all ingredients together. The spinach will be cooked just enough from the heat of the other ingredients.
10) Serve with garlic/herb bread.

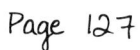

Vegetable Lasagne

Serves 5-6

A delicious adaptation of the traditional beef and pasta dish. Try serving it with a light salad, e.g. Mostly Green Salad (page 69).

creative tip: You can vary the vegetables in this dish, add beans or lentils or even TVP if you like the mock meat version. If you like soy cheese, add it to the bechamel sauce for a stronger cheesy flavour.

Vegetable and tomato sauce
1 large onion, finely chopped
1 tbsp. olive oil
1 capsicum, diced
3 large cloves garlic, crushed
810g tin crushed tomatoes
2 tsp. dried oregano
3 tbsp. tomato paste
2 tbsp. tamari sauce
Freshly ground black pepper, to season
8 heaped cups vegetables chopped into small pieces*
½ cup fresh chopped basil leaves

Béchamel sauce
1 tub tofu cream cheese (227g)
2 large cloves garlic, crushed
2 tbsp. savoury yeast flakes
1 cup soy or rice milk
1 ½ tbsp. ground arrowroot

Extras
2 packets 250g instant lasagne sheets
Grated soy cheese or breadcrumbs for topping

*A food processor is good for chopping the vegetables very small. The lasagne sits better this way and there is a real melding of flavours.

1) In a large saucepan, stir fry the onion in olive oil until tender.
2) Add the capsicum, and cook for a further 2—3 minutes.
3) Add the garlic, tomatoes, oregano, tomato paste and tamari sauce. Simmer covered for 10 minutes. Make sure you stir occasionally.
4) Meanwhile, pre-heat oven to 180°C. Then in a blender or food processor, combine the béchamel sauce ingredients.
5) When the tomato sauce is ready, remove from heat and season with pepper, then stir in the vegetables and basil.
6) Take a large baking dish (32cm x 24cm) and line with sheets of lasagne.
7) Spoon a thin layer of vegetable sauce over the pasta sheets and then top with a thin layer of béchamel sauce and another layer of pasta. Continue this way until you run out of ingredients. You should run out of the vegetable sauce first. If you can find a good soy cheese, it will finish the lasagne off nicely and will be closer to the authentic taste. However breadcrumbs provide a crunchy finish as well.
8) Bake the lasagne for 40-50 minutes. When you push a knife through the pasta, it should easily slide through.
9) Serve hot with salads of your choice.

Roasted Capsicum Pasta

Serves 4

A delicious pasta sauce, rich in flavour and made with oven-baked ingredients.

creative tip — This sauce is also a good dip or sauce over roasted vegetables. It makes a nice addition to pizza sauces too.

2 medium-sized onions, peeled
5 large red capsicums
4 medium-sized tomatoes (approx. 600g)
1 whole head garlic
2 tbsp. olive oil or olive oil spray
½ tsp. sea salt
500g of your favourite pasta

1) Pre-heat oven to 180°C.
2) Cut the onions into quarters and the capsicums and tomatoes in halves. Remove the cores. Leave the head of garlic as it is.
4) Place all vegetables (including garlic) into two oven-proof dishes and drizzle (or spray) olive oil over the top. Sprinkle on the salt.
5) Bake for 50 minutes. During this time, check to see whether any of the vegetables are charred. If they are, remove them and put the others back into the oven. The garlic will take approximately 30 minutes and should not be left longer. When vegetables are done, they should all be soft and slightly charred.
6) Once the vegetables are cooked, bring some water to the boil in a large saucepan and add the pasta. Cook until tender.
8) Push the garlic cloves out of their skins and puree with the rest of the vegetables until smooth.
9) Serve the sauce over hot pasta.

Satay Vegetables & Soba Noodles

Serves 4

This dish combines the flavours of tomato and satay with noodles and vegetables. This version is quite mild. For a spicier dish, add a couple more chillies.

250g soba noodles
1 red onion, chopped
1 tbsp. sesame oil
2 small red chillies, seeded and finely chopped
2 large cloves garlic, crushed
1 x 415g tin crushed tomatoes
4 tbsp. smooth peanut butter
½ cup water
1 vegetable stock cube
3 sprigs fresh thyme
1 large carrot, chopped (approx. 180g)
125g baby corn, chopped
1 medium-sized zucchini, chopped (approx. 250g)
1 capsicum, chopped
200g broccoli, chopped

1) Add soba noodles to boiling water and stir often to make sure they don't stick together. They only take a few minutes to cook. Once they are done, drain, rinse and set aside.
2) Meanwhile, in a wok or large saucepan, stir fry onion in sesame oil until tender.
3) Add chilli and garlic, and stir fry for 1 minute.
4) Add tomatoes, peanut butter, water and stock cube and stir until smooth. Simmer for 5 minutes.
5) Add the leaves from thyme sprigs, carrot and corn, and simmer for 5 minutes.
6) Add remaining vegetables and simmer until just tender (3–5 minutes).
7) Add the noodles to the vegetable mix, and stir over medium heat until they are well coated and hot. (Note: check to make sure the noodles are not stuck together before you add them. If they are, submerge in hot water or rinse and break apart.)

Pad Thai

Serves 4

This is an adaptation of the traditional Thai dish that usually contains egg and fish sauce. This version uses tofu as a replacement for the egg and a variety of fresh, zesty flavours to create an experience not far from the real thing.

1 large carrot (approx. 180g)
1 tbsp. ground arrowroot
150g silken tofu
3 tbsp. tomato paste
¼ cup water
1 tbsp. unrefined brown sugar
3 tbsp. rice mirin
2 tbsp. tamari sauce
1 tbsp. lime juice
½ tbsp. tamarind paste
250g flat rice noodles
1 tbsp. sesame oil
4 spring onions, finely chopped
1 small red chilli, seeded and finely chopped
3 large cloves garlic, crushed
1 tbsp. fresh grated ginger
1 tablespoon fresh chopped lemongrass
1 very full cup chopped broccoli
3 cups bean sprouts
1 cup fresh finely chopped coriander
100g crushed peanuts
lime wedges to serve

Note: This dish needs to be cooked quickly and then served straight away. For this reason, it is important to have all ingredients measured and ready before beginning to cook. The method is set out in a series of individual steps to prepare all of *the separate components of the dish, including the vegetables, the sauce and the tofu mixture.*

1) Use a peeler to grate the carrot into large, thin slices. It is best not to grate it with a traditional grater as the pieces will be too small.
2) In a small bowl with an electric mixer, or in a food processor, combine the arrowroot and tofu until it forms a smooth paste.
3) In another small bowl, combine tomato paste, water, brown sugar, rice mirin, tamari sauce, lime juice and tamarind paste.
4) Cook rice noodles according to directions on the packet and then strain.
5) Once all of the above mixtures and ingredients are ready and set out for easy access, and the additional ingredients in the list are measured, you are ready to begin cooking. In a wok, heat the sesame oil.
6) Add the spring onions, chilli, garlic, ginger and lemongrass. Stir fry over low heat being careful not to burn.
7) Add the sauce mixture (tomato paste, tamari sauce etc.)
8) Allow sauce to simmer for a couple of minutes.
9) Add the tofu mixture and stir into the sauce. The mixture should start to thicken.
10) Add the carrot and broccoli, and simmer for another couple of minutes.
11) Remove from heat and add the rice noodles and bean sprouts. Toss all ingredients until well combined and return to heat.
12) Once the mixture is hot, remove from heat and add the coriander. Mix well and serve immediately, sprinkled with crushed peanuts and with lime wedges on the side.

Cashew Soba Noodles

Serves 4

This is an Asian-style noodle stir fry, rich in flavour and open to variation. Feel free to substitute any of the vegetables or even the type of noodle you use.

2 tbsp. fresh grated ginger
1½ tbsp. white wine vinegar or rice mirin
½ cup cashews
2 tbsp. tamari sauce
1 tbsp. rice syrup
2 tbsp. water
1 cup fresh chopped coriander
250g soba noodles
1 tbsp. sesame oil
1 onion, sliced into rings
3 large cloves garlic, crushed
2 small chillies, seeded and finely chopped
1 medium-sized carrot, chopped (approx. 100g)
1 cup chopped baby corn
200g broccoli, chopped
1 cup chopped mushrooms

1) In a blender, process ginger, vinegar or rice mirin, cashews, tamari sauce, rice syrup, water and coriander. Set aside.
2) Add soba noodles to boiling water and stir often to make sure they don't stick together. They only take a few minutes to cook. Once they are done, drain and set aside.
3) Heat sesame oil in a wok and stir fry onions until tender.
4) Add garlic and chilli and stir fry for 1 minute.
5) Add carrots and baby corn. If vegetables are sticking to the pan, add a little extra water.
6) After 5 minutes, add broccoli and mushrooms, and stir fry for a few minutes.
7) Stir sauce into vegetable mixture and return to heat to simmer for 5 minutes, stirring often.
8) Remove from heat and add noodles. Stir until well combined and then return to heat for a short time until mixture is hot enough to serve.

Roasted Pumpkin Fried Rice

Serves 4

For lovers of pumpkin and pinenuts, this is a great, light meal.

1 vegetable stock cube
3 cups hot water
2 cups white rice
600g peeled pumpkin
1 tsp. black peppercorns
2 tbsp. olive oil
juice of 1 lemon
3 cloves garlic (unpeeled)
100g pine nuts
4 spring onions
1 tbsp. olive oil, extra
1 cup fresh chopped basil

1) Pre-heat oven to 180°C and then dissolve stock cube in the water. You may need to do this on the stove.
2) Rinse rice and boil in the stock water until most of the water has been absorbed. Leave to stand.
3) Meanwhile, chop pumpkin into small cubes.
4) Roughly crush the peppercorns in a mortar and pestle.
5) In a large bowl, combine olive oil, three quarters of the lemon juice and peppercorns.
6) Add the pumpkin to the dressing and stir until well coated.
7) Place pumpkin and unpeeled garlic into a baking dish and bake for 30 minutes.
8) Place pinenuts onto a tray and roast in the oven for 5 minutes or until just browned (be careful not to burn them).
9) In a large frying pan or wok, stir fry spring onions in extra olive oil until tender.
10) Peel and mash the baked garlic and add to the onions with the pumpkin. Stir until well combined.
11) Add the rice and stir over medium heat for a few minutes.
12) Before serving stir in the basil, pinenuts, and remaining lemon juice.

Wild Fried Rice

Serves 4-5

A modern fried rice with roasted vegetables, rosemary and lime.

2 cups brown rice
½ cup wild rice
1 large potato, scrubbed (approx. 300g)
500g sweet potatoes, peeled
1 large carrot, scrubbed (approx. 180g)
1-2 tbsp. olive oil
1 tbsp. mixed herbs
1 cup chopped broccoli
1 red onion, roughly chopped
1 tbsp olive oil, extra
3 tbsp. tamari sauce
1 tbsp. rice mirin
2 tbsp. lime juice
1 tbsp. balsamic vinegar
6 stems fresh rosemary
1 cup chopped green beans
1 red capsicum, roughly chopped

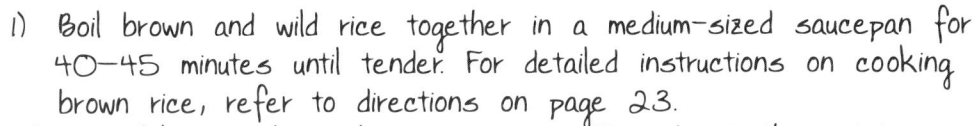

1) Boil brown and wild rice together in a medium-sized saucepan for 40-45 minutes until tender. For detailed instructions on cooking brown rice, refer to directions on page 23.
2) Meanwhile, pre-heat the oven to 180°C and cut the potato, sweet potato and carrot into chunks (a little larger than bite size).
3) Put the vegetables you just cut into a large mixing bowl with the olive oil and mixed herbs. Stir until all vegetables are coated.
4) Place vegetables onto a baking tray and bake for 30-40 minutes or until tender. Baking time will depend on the size of your vegetable pieces.
5) Steam broccoli until just tender.
6) When rice is ready, stir fry the onion with the extra olive oil in a large wok or frying pan until tender, then add rices.
7) Add roast vegetables and remaining ingredients. Mix well and cook for a further 5-10 minutes, stirring often. Serve hot.

Vegetable Pilau

Serves 4

A tasty rice dish filled with Indian spices.

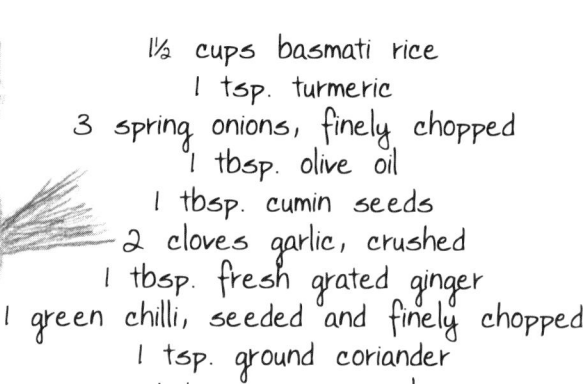

1½ cups basmati rice
1 tsp. turmeric
3 spring onions, finely chopped
1 tbsp. olive oil
1 tbsp. cumin seeds
2 cloves garlic, crushed
1 tbsp. fresh grated ginger
1 green chilli, seeded and finely chopped
1 tsp. ground coriander
1 tsp. garam masala
1 tsp. ground paprika
4 cups of your favourite vegetables*, chopped small
5 tbsp. soy yoghurt
¼ cup fresh finely chopped coriander
1 tbsp. fresh finely chopped mint
1 tbsp. tomato paste
pinch of sea salt
juice of ½ lemon

*e.g. carrots, peas, beans, baby corn, mushrooms, cauliflower

1) Cook the rice according to directions on page 22, but add the turmeric to the water. This will make it a golden colour when cooked.
2) Meanwhile, in a large frying pan, stir fry the spring onions in the oil.
3) Remove from heat and add the cumin seeds, garlic, ginger, chilli and spices then return to heat and stir well for 1 minute.
4) Add the vegetables and stir to coat in the seasonings. At this stage, have a cup of water standing by and add a little if needed to keep the pan moist.
5) In a small bowl, combine the remaining ingredients (except rice).
6) When vegetables are starting to become tender, add the rice and mix well. Keep stirring over the heat for a few minutes.
7) Add the yoghurt mixture. Stir until it is evenly distributed throughout the rice then serve.

Mediterranean Vegetable Risotto

Serves 4

This risotto is just as creamy and flavoursome as those filled with cheese. I recommend the vegetable pieces be cut very small.

creative tip: Risotto really needs to be eaten as soon as it is cooked as the texture changes. But if you have any leftovers make small patties and roll them in breadcrumbs. Fry them on both sides and serve with salad. They are delicious!

800ml water
1 vegetable stock cube
1 tbsp. olive oil
1 tbsp. vegan margarine
1 onion, finely chopped
3 cloves garlic, crushed
2 cups Arborio rice
½ cup white wine
1 cup cubed pumpkin
1 cup chopped capsicum
1 cup diced tomato
1 cup chopped zucchini
1 cup chopped mushrooms
7 finely chopped sun-dried tomatoes
2 tbsp. soy cream cheese
½ cup fresh chopped basil
freshly ground black pepper, to season

1) Bring water to boil in a small saucepan and then add the stock cube. Stir to dissolve.
2) Leave the stock simmering and heat the oil and margarine in a separate large saucepan.
3) Add the onion and garlic to the oil and stir-fry until the onion is just tender.
4) Add the rice and stir for one minute. Keep the heat on medium-low.
5) Add the wine and pumpkin and stir until the wine is absorbed.

6) Using a ladle, add the stock a little at a time. Do not add more stock until each addition is absorbed and stir often to prevent the rice sticking and to create a creamy texture.
7) When ¾ of the stock has been added to the rice, add remaining vegetables including the sun-dried tomatoes. Mix well.
8) Before serving, stir in the cream cheese and basil and season with pepper. Serve immediately with a salad and/or warm bread.

"Men dig their graves with their own teeth and die more by those fated instruments than the weapons of their enemies"
***Thomas Moffet* Health's Improvement, 1600 A.D.**

Sauces & Dips

Sauces & Dips

Then God said, "I give you every seed-bearing plant on the face of the whole earth and every tree that has fruit with seed in it. They will be yours for food...."
Genesis 1:29-30 New International Version (NIV)

Cashew & Pepper Gravy

Makes 400ml

This delicious gravy goes well with roasted vegetables, burgers and Lentil Loaf (see page 115).

½ onion, very finely chopped
½ tbsp. olive oil
2 cloves garlic, crushed
1½ cups water
1 tsp. dried tarragon
1 tbsp. tamari sauce
1 tsp. whole peppercorns
½ cup unsalted cashews
1 tbsp. ground arrowroot
¼ cup water, extra

Sauces & Dips

1) In a small saucepan, stir fry the onion in olive oil until tender.
2) Add the garlic and mix well.
3) Add the water, tarragon and tamari sauce and bring to the boil.
4) Meanwhile, crush the peppercorns using a mortar and pestle or grinder, and process the cashews in a food processor.
5) Add to the saucepan and simmer for 10 minutes.
6) In a cup, stir the ground arrowroot into the extra water until completely smooth.
7) Add the ground arrowroot mixture to the gravy whilst stirring constantly. It should thicken right away.
8) Serve hot over vegetables or burgers.

Make sure your peppercorns are freshly crushed

Peanut Sauce

Makes 400ml

Peanut sauce adds flavour to anything: vegetables, burgers, rice and salad. You don't have to include the chilli either, it is just there to add a bit of a kick.

4 cloves garlic, crushed
1 small red chilli, seeded and finely chopped
1 tbsp. sesame or peanut oil
½ cup natural crunchy peanut butter
1½ cups coconut milk
2 tbsp. tamari sauce
2 tsp. brown sugar
1 tbsp. lemon juice

1) In a medium-sized saucepan, stir fry the garlic and chilli in the oil for one minute.
2) Remove from heat and add remaining ingredients.
3) Return to heat and stir until smooth. This sauce is quite thick, as you will see at this stage. If you prefer a runny sauce, add more coconut milk or some water.
4) Leave to simmer on a low heat for 10 minutes, stirring occasionally.
5) Serve warm or cool.

Sauces & Dips

Fresh Tomato Sauce

Makes approximately 750ml

The pumpkin seeds really add to the taste and texture of this sauce and it goes well over roasted vegetables or with pasta.

1 onion, chopped
1 tbsp. olive oil
3 cloves garlic, crushed
1 red capsicum, chopped
6 large tomatoes, diced (approx. 900g)
5 tbsp. tomato paste
2 tsp. dried mixed herbs
½ cup pumpkin seeds
sea salt, to season
handful of fresh basil leaves

Sauces & Dips

1) In a large saucepan, stir fry the onion in olive oil until tender.
2) Add the garlic and capsicum, and mix well.
3) Add the tomatoes, tomato paste and herbs, and simmer for at least half an hour with the lid on, stirring occasionally.
4) Dry-roast the pumpkin seeds in a small saucepan.
5) Right before serving, season with salt and tear the basil leaves up and add to the sauce with the pumpkin seeds.

Barbecue Sauce

Makes 600ml

This is a rich and tasty sauce that goes well with vegetables, beans and burgers.

1 medium-sized onion, roughly chopped
1 tbsp. olive oil
5 medium-sized tomatoes, diced (approx. 750g)
3 large cloves garlic, crushed
½ cup apple juice
2 tbsp. tamari sauce
1 tsp. dried thyme
½ tbsp. Dijon mustard
1 tbsp. apple cider vinegar
1 tbsp. tomato paste
1 tbsp. blackstrap molasses

1) In a medium-sized saucepan, stir fry the onion in olive oil until tender.
2) Add the tomatoes and garlic and leave to simmer over low heat until the tomatoes are mushy. Stir occasionally to make sure that nothing sticks to the pan.
3) Add the remaining ingredients and stir well.
4) Simmer for 15 minutes over low heat, with the lid on, stirring occasionally.
5) Remove from heat and leave to cool.
6) Puree in a food processor or blender until smooth.
7) Serve warm or at room temperature.

Pizza Sauce

Covers 2 x 36cm pizza bases

Try making this pizza sauce instead of using plain old tomato paste on your pizzas. It may require more effort but it is definitely worth it! Make double and freeze it for later.

1 onion, roughly chopped
1 tbsp. olive oil
3 cloves garlic, crushed
5 medium-sized tomatoes, roughly chopped (approx. 750g)
¼ tsp mixed spice
¼ tsp. sea salt
1 tsp. dried oregano
3 tsp. rice syrup or unrefined sugar
2 tbsp. tomato paste
handful of fresh basil leaves

Sauces & Dips

1) In a medium-sized saucepan, stir fry the onion in olive oil until tender.
2) Add all remaining ingredients except basil and mix well.
3) Leave to simmer with the lid on over low heat for 20 minutes. Stir often.
4) Remove the sauce from heat, tear the basil leaves up and stir into the sauce.
5) Leave to cool and then puree in a blender or food processor.
6) Spread over your pizza bases.

Asian Dipping Sauce

This is a sweet sauce to go with rice balls and spring rolls. If you like your sauces hot, add a finely chopped chilli.

1 tbsp. tamari sauce
1 tbsp. rice mirin
1 tsp. unrefined sugar
1 tsp. fresh grated ginger
1 tsp. sesame oil

1) Combine all ingredients in a small dish and serve.

Mint Dipping Sauce

Makes ¾ cup

This sauce is a great cooler for anything spicy. Serve it with curries or with hors d' oeuvre.

¼ cup fresh mint leaves
½ cup soy yoghurt
1 tsp. lemon juice
Pinch of sea salt
2 tsp. unrefined sugar

1) Chop the mint finely, then combine with the remaining ingredients, or, blend all ingredients in a food processor.
2) Serve chilled in a small serving dish.

Tomato Salsa

Salsa goes well with any Mexican food but can also be used as a dip. If you are making it as a dip, use a food processor rather than chopping the ingredients by hand for a smoother dip texture.

1 small red onion
1 small bunch of fresh coriander (approx. 40g)
1 medium-sized red chilli, seeded
1 capsicum
5 medium-sized tomatoes (approx. 750g), diced
3 cloves garlic, crushed
1 tbsp. ground cumin
3 tbsp. lime juice
pinch of sea salt

1) Gather the onion, coriander, chilli and capsicum and either chop very finely, or combine in a food processor.
2) Put chopped ingredients into a medium-sized mixing bowl and add the remaining ingredients. Mix well.
3) Garnish with coriander and serve with Mexican food or as a dip.

Baba Ganoush

A Mediterranean dip based on eggplant. This goes well with warm pita bread and raw vegetables sticks or try adding it to a salad sandwich. The eggplant does not need bleeding in this recipe.

1 medium-sized eggplant
juice of ½ lemon
¼ cup tahini
1 large clove garlic, crushed
2 tbsp. fresh chopped parsley
1 tbsp. olive oil

1) Pre-heat oven to 180°C, then prick the eggplant with a knife in a few different places and place onto a baking tray.
2) Bake in the oven for approximately 40 minutes or until soft.
3) Peel the eggplant and puree in a food processor with the remaining ingredients until smooth.

Homous

A traditional, Middle Eastern dip made of chickpeas and tahini. It is great served with raw vegetables or Lebanese bread.

creative tip: For different flavoured homous varieties, add any one of the following: roasted capsicum, fresh coriander, fresh parsley, Indian pickle or a pinch of cayenne pepper.

1 cup dried chick peas (2½ cups cooked)
¾ cup tahini
juice of 1 medium-sized lemon
½ cup water
2 cloves garlic, crushed
3 tbsp. cold pressed olive oil
½ tsp. sea salt

1) If you are using dried chickpeas, prepare them according to directions on page 19 and then allow to cool.
2) Blend all ingredients together in a food processor until smooth.

Serving Suggestion
Lebanese Bread
vege sticks
crackers

Sauces & Dips

Refreshing Guacamole

This guacamole is light and refreshing thanks to the addition of cucumber and it has the added sweetness of the corn and tomato to make it a little different.

½ tbsp. olive oil
1 cup corn kernels
1 small bunch of fresh coriander (approx. 40g)
2 spring onions
3 medium-sized avocados
1 tsp. balsamic vinegar
10-12cm piece of cucumber
3 cloves garlic, crushed
juice of ½ a lemon
1 medium-sized tomato, diced (approx. 150g)

1) In a frying pan, heat the olive oil and then stir fry the corn kernels until browned. Set aside.
2) Mix the coriander and spring onions in a food processor.
3) Once they are finely chopped, add the avocado flesh, vinegar, cucumber, garlic and lemon juice and mix to a creamy puree.
4) Stir in the tomato and corn kernels and serve with Mexican food or as a dip.

Sauces & Dips

Roasted Capsicum & Cashew Pesto

This pesto may be used as a dip or a pasta sauce. It is yummy served with thin crackers, warm baguette slices or vegetable sticks.

3 large red capsicums
olive oil to drizzle
½ head whole garlic
½ cup basil leaves (firmly packed)
¼ cup chopped rocket leaves (firmly packed)
200g unsalted cashews
pinch of sea salt

1) Pre-heat oven to 180°C.
2) Cut capsicums and remove seeds and cores.
3) Place capsicums into a baking dish and drizzle with olive oil. Add unpeeled garlic to the dish.
4) Bake for 30 – 45 minutes (until capsicum starts to char). Remove garlic after 30 minutes.
5) Remove garlic cloves from their skins and puree with the capsicums and remaining ingredients.
6) Serve at room temperature.

"It's not the killing of the animals that is the chief issue here, but rather the unspeakable quality of the lives they are forced to live."
From the book Diet for a new America. Copyright 1987 by John Robbins

reprinted with permission of HJ Kramer/New World Library, Novato, CA

Baked Goodies

Vegan Baking Tips

Some of the tips below are helpful for regular baking and some are specific to recipes without eggs. This section of the book has been the most challenging because I am used to a very relaxed and nonspecific style of cooking. I learned however that baking has to be specific. It is a science and each recipe is a very exact formula, which if not followed precisely, can have very altered results.

General rules to follow when baking

- When mixing cakes, be careful not to overmix as mixing stimulates the gluten in the flour and gives the cake a more rubbery texture.
- Measure ingredients exactly.
- For best results bring chilled ingredients to room temperature before using so that the temperature of a batter or dough is even.
- Pre-heat the oven to the exact temperature to ensure that the item is cooked evenly and constantly for the required time.
- Put cakes and muffins into the oven as soon as they are mixed as the leavening (rising) agent starts working right away and it is best if this occurs in the oven.
- Make sure that biscuits and muffins are a consistent size so that they cook evenly.
- Vegan cakes take longer to cook than those with eggs. For this reason it is best not to use deep cake tins. If you would like a deeper cake, use two sandwich tins and put the cakes together with icing.
- Wait until vegan cakes are cool before cutting them.
- Resist the urge to open the oven before the cake is at least ¾ of the way through the required cooking time. Otherwise the middle will sink.

Chocolate Coconut Biscuits

Makes 12 large biscuits

These biscuits are just sweet and rich enough to satisfy that chocolate craving!

¼ cup sunflower oil
½ cup pure maple syrup
½ tsp. baking powder
6 tbsp. cocoa
1 cup plain wholemeal flour
½ cup desiccated coconut

1) Pre-heat oven to 180°C and grease a large baking tray.
2) In a medium-sized mixing bowl, whisk oil and maple syrup.
3) Add remaining ingredients and mix well. The mixture will be wet and sticky.
4) Shape mixture into balls and flatten onto the baking tray. Make them about 7cm in diameter.
5) Bake 10–12 minutes, taking care not to burn. Leave to cool and harden on a rack before eating.

Cinnamon Biscuits

Makes 20

These are crunchy little treats!

creative tip: Instead of cinnamon you can use mixed spice or ginger. These biscuits are also nice half-dipped in melted chocolate.

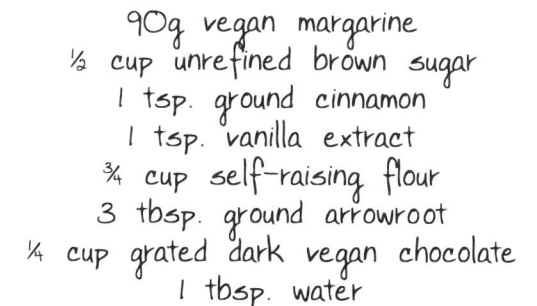

90g vegan margarine
½ cup unrefined brown sugar
1 tsp. ground cinnamon
1 tsp. vanilla extract
¾ cup self-raising flour
3 tbsp. ground arrowroot
¼ cup grated dark vegan chocolate
1 tbsp. water

1) Pre-heat oven to 180°C and grease a large baking tray.
2) In a medium-sized mixing bowl, cream the margarine and sugar.
3) In a separate bowl, mix the remaining ingredients except the water.
4) Gradually add to the wet mixture using the water when it gets too dry. The consistency should be a firm dough.
5) Roll out on a floured surface to 2-3 millimetres thick.
6) Cut into small circles with a cookie cutter.
7) Bake 10-12 minutes making sure you remove from the oven before they start to darken. Leave to cool and harden on a rack before eating.

Oat & Malt Biscuits

Makes 25

I used an Anzac biscuit recipe as a base for these, but developed it into a healthier version with the unique taste of malt.

creative tip

Try adding your choice of dried fruit and or nuts to this recipe.

1 cup plain wholemeal flour
¾ cup desiccated coconut
½ cup unrefined sugar
1 cup rolled oats
125g vegan margarine
2 tbsp. barley malt
1 tsp. bicarbonate of soda
1 tbsp. water

1) Pre-heat oven to 170°C and grease a large baking tray.
2) In a medium-sized mixing bowl, combine the dry ingredients.
3) In a small saucepan, melt the margarine and barley malt until smooth.
4) Stir in the bicarbonate of soda.
5) Add the margarine mixture and water to the dry ingredients and mix well.
6) Shape heaped teaspoons of mixture into balls and press onto the baking tray. Bake 18–20 minutes. Leave to cool and harden on a rack before eating.

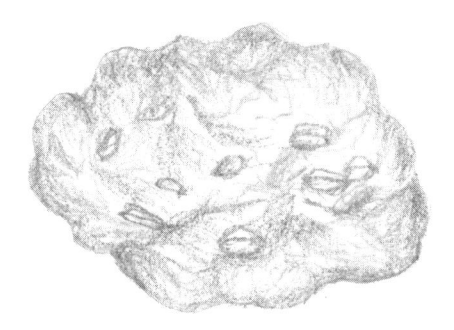

Peanut Butter Biscuits

Makes 15

These biscuits are crunchy and very peanutty.

creative tip: Chocolate chips are a great addition to this recipe. Or if you prefer you can use other nut butters.

¼ cup vegan margarine
5 tbsp. brown sugar (firmly packed)
5 tbsp. crunchy peanut butter
½ tsp. vanilla extract
1½ tbsp. soy milk
¾ cup plain flour
¼ cup ground arrowroot
½ tsp. baking powder
pinch of salt

1) Pre-heat oven to 180°C and grease a large baking tray.
2) In a medium-sized mixing bowl, cream the margarine, sugar and peanut butter until smooth.
3) Add the vanilla and soy milk and mix well.
4) In a separate bowl combine remaining ingredients.
5) Gradually add the flour mixture to the wet ingredients. The mixture will eventually become a stiff dough.
6) Form the mixture into balls and press down on the baking tray. Flatten with a fork.
7) Bake for 10-15 mins (until lightly browned). Leave to cool and harden on a rack before eating.

Passion Stars

Makes 30

These are small, star-shaped biscuits that have a passionfruit and vanilla flavour.

125g vegan margarine
½ cup unrefined sugar
1 tsp. vanilla extract
pulp from 2 large passionfruit
1 cup plain flour
¼ cup ground arrowroot

1) Grease 2 baking trays.
2) In a medium-sized mixing bowl, cream the margarine, sugar and vanilla.
3) Add the passionfruit and mix well.
4) Add remaining ingredients and knead to a smooth dough.
5) Roll out on a floured surface to ½cm thick and cut with a star-shaped cookie cutter.
6) Place onto trays and refrigerate for 20 minutes.
7) Pre-heat oven to 180°C.
8) Bake biscuits for 15-20 minutes, until they go golden. Leave to cool and harden on a rack before eating.

Actual size

American Style Choc Chip Cookies

Makes 20

These are crunchy on the outside and slightly chewy in the middle. If you prefer them to be crunchy all the way through, leave them in the oven for a couple of minutes longer.

1 cup plus 2 tbsp. plain flour
½ tsp. bicarbonate of soda
pinch of salt
½ cup vegan margarine (at room temperature)
6 tbsp. brown sugar
5 tbsp. unrefined sugar
1½ tsp vanilla extract
2 tbsp. soy milk
½ cup choc chips

1) Pre-heat the oven to 175°C and grease a large baking tray.
2) In a small mixing bowl, combine all of the flour, bicarbonate of soda and salt.
3) In a larger bowl, cream the margarine and sugars with an electric mixer until very creamy.
4) Add the vanilla and milk and mix well.
5) Slowly add the flour to the wet ingredients, mixing by hand.
6) Fold in the choc chips and mix to a firm dough.
7) Form mixture into small balls and press onto the baking tray.
8) Bake for 10-12 minutes (the cookies should be golden brown). Leave to cool and harden on a rack before eating.

♥ sweet, crunchy, slightly chewy, chocolatey morsels ♥

Lemon Coconut Biscuits

Makes 20

These are light crunchy biscuits with the flavours of lemon, coconut and vanilla.

5½ tbsp. vegan margarine
½ cup unrefined sugar
1 tsp. vanilla extract
½ cup desiccated coconut
2 tsp. finely grated lemon rind
¾ cup self-raising flour
¼ cup ground arrowroot
2 tbsp. lemon juice

1) Pre-heat the oven to 175°C and grease a large baking tray.
2) In a medium-sized mixing bowl, cream the margarine and sugar with an electric mixer until very creamy.
3) Add the vanilla and mix well.
4) Stir in the coconut, and lemon rind.
5) Add the remaining ingredients and mix to a dough – you will need to use your hands to press the ingredients together.
6) Form mixture into balls and press onto the baking tray. Press down with a fork, first one way and then across the other way so that the biscuit is decorated with crosses.
7) Bake for 10-12 minutes (the biscuits should be golden brown). Leave to cool and harden on a rack before eating.

Baked Goodies

Chocolate Brownies

These moist, chocolaty brownies are a great sugar free treat. Feel free to vary the type of nuts you use in the recipe. Hazelnuts and almonds are also good.

¼ cup vegetable oil
½ cup pure maple syrup
½ cup soy yoghurt (plain or vanilla)
1 cup self-raising flour
¼ cup cocoa
100g vegan chocolate (at room temp.)
100g chopped walnuts

1) Pre-heat oven to 180°C and grease a 26cm x 16cm lamington tin. (a lamington tin is similar to a Swiss roll or brownie tin).
2) In a medium-sized mixing bowl, whisk the oil, maple syrup and yoghurt until smooth.
3) Sift in the flour and cocoa, and mix well.
4) Grate or crush the chocolate, and add to the mixture gradually until it is consistent.
5) Stir in the walnuts.
6) Pour mixture into the tin and spread evenly over the bottom.
7) Bake for 25 minutes or until a skewer comes out clean when tested. Cool on a rack and then cut into squares.

Baked Goodies

Dream for a chocoholic...

Banana & Walnut Muffins

Makes 12

These are a delicious snack for morning or afternoon tea, especially served warm with vegan margarine.

1 cup wholemeal self-raising flour
1 cup plain self-raising flour
pinch of sea salt
2 tsp. baking powder
1 tsp. mixed spice
100g crushed walnuts
¾ cup pure maple syrup
1 cup mashed banana
2 tsp. vanilla extract
½ cup rice or soy milk
2 tbsp. sunflower oil

1) Pre-heat oven to 180°C and prepare a muffin tin.
2) In a large mixing bowl, sift flour and add the salt, baking powder, mixed spice and walnuts. Mix well.
3) In a blender or with an electric mixer, combine the maple syrup, banana, vanilla and milk.
4) Add to the dry ingredients and mix gently until smooth.
5) Add the oil and blend slowly until mixed in.
6) Spoon mixture into the muffin tin and bake for 12–15 minutes or until a skewer comes out clean when tested.

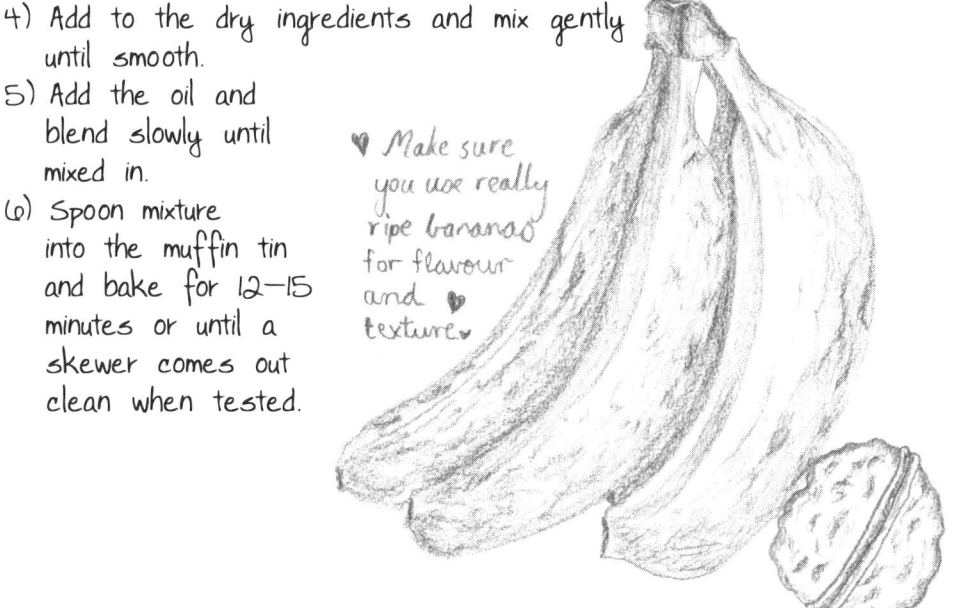

♥ Make sure you use really ripe bananas for flavour and texture ♥

Apple & Cinnamon Muffins

Makes 10-12

These muffins are sweet and moist.

220g self-raising flour
1 tsp. baking powder
1½ tsp. ground cinnamon
120g vegan margarine
½ cup unrefined sugar
1½ tsp. vanilla extract
1 cup unsweetened applesauce or stewed apple

1) Pre-heat oven to 180°C and prepare a muffin tin.
2) Place flour, baking powder and cinnamon into a medium sized mixing bowl and mix well.
3) In a separate larger mixing bowl, cream the margarine and sugar with an electric mixer until it is very light in colour.
4) Add the vanilla and apple and mix well.
5) Slowly add the dry ingredients to the wet, stirring gently by hand.
6) Spoon into the muffin tin and bake for 25-30 minutes or until a skewer comes out clean when tested.
7) Leave to cool in the tin for 10 minutes before transferring to a wire cooling rack.

Berry Chocolate Muffins

Makes 12

Berry chocolaty and berry nice!

2 cups self-raising flour
1 tbsp. soy flour
½ cup cocoa
1 tsp. baking powder
1 cup unrefined sugar
160ml vegetable oil
1 tsp. vanilla extract
160ml rice or soy milk
160ml apple juice
1 cup mixed frozen berries

1) Pre-heat oven to 180°C and prepare a muffin tin.
2) In a large mixing bowl, sift flours and cocoa, then add the baking powder and sugar.
3) In a separate, smaller bowl, whisk the vegetable oil, vanilla, milk and apple juice.
4) Slowly stir the combined wet ingredients into the dry ingredients, then stir in the berries.
5) Spoon into the muffin tin and bake for 30-35 minutes or until a skewer comes out clean when tested.
6) Leave to cool in the tin for 10 minutes before transferring to a wire cooling rack.

Baked Goodies

The cross-section of a warm Berry Chocolate muffin!

Date Loaf

This is a simple but tasty cake. A great afternoon tea snack served warm.

1 cup very finely chopped dates
¼ cup vegan margarine
½ cup unrefined brown sugar
1 tsp. bicarbonate of soda
1 tsp. vanilla extract
1 cup boiling water
1¾ cups self-raising flour
½ tsp. mixed spice

1) Pre-heat oven to 180°C, then grease and line a 25cm x 13cm loaf tin.
2) In a medium-sized mixing bowl, combine the dates, margarine, sugar, bicarbonate of soda and boiling water. Stir until margarine has melted.
3) Add the vanilla then gently stir in the flour and mixed spice until well combined.
4) Pour into the loaf tin and bake for 35 minutes or until a skewer comes out clean when tested.

Baked Goodies

Blueberry Cake

The blueberries need to be frozen for this recipe so that they don't get squashed during the mixing

120g vegan margarine
½ cup unrefined sugar
1½ tsp. vanilla extract
1 cup unsweetened applesauce or stewed apple
220g self-raising flour
1 tsp. baking powder
½ cup frozen blueberries

1) Pre-heat oven to 180°C and grease and line a 19cm round cake tin.
2) In a large mixing bowl, cream the margarine and sugar with an electric mixer until it is very light in colour.
3) Add the vanilla and apple and mix well.
4) Slowly add the flour and baking powder to the wet ingredients, stirring gently by hand.
5) Lastly, stir in the blueberries. Note the mixture will be thick.
6) Pour into the cake tin making sure there is an even coverage. Bake for 40-45 minutes or until a skewer comes out clean when tested.
7) Leave to cool in the tin for 10 minutes before transferring to a wire cooing rack.

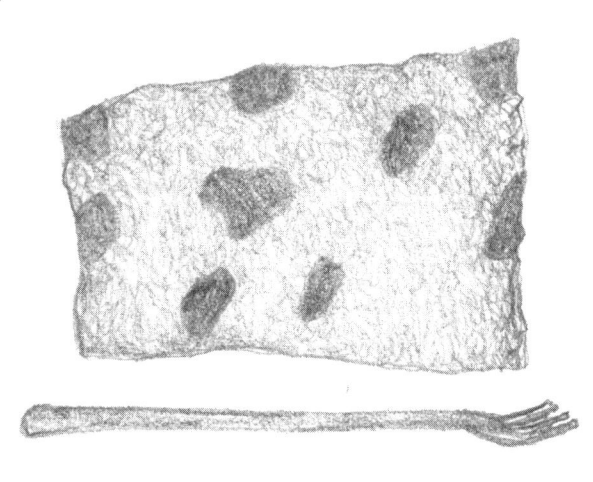

Chocolate Cake

This is a rich, moist, chocolate double decker cake.

Cake
3 cups self-raising flour
¾ cup cocoa
2 tsp. baking powder
1½ cups unrefined sugar
1 cup vegetable oil
1 tsp. vanilla extract
1 cup rice or soy milk
1 cup apple juice
2 tbsp. apple cider vinegar

Icing
350g silken tofu
6 tbsp. cocoa
200g vegan chocolate

1) Pre-heat oven to 180°C and grease and line two 17cm sandwich cake tins.
2) In a large mixing bowl, sift flour and cocoa, and then add the baking powder and sugar. Mix well.
3) In a separate, smaller bowl, whisk the vegetable oil, vanilla, milk and apple juice.
4) Slowly stir the combined wet ingredients into the dry ingredients.
5) Right before baking, mix in the apple cider vinegar.
6) Pour into the cake tins and bake for 30-35 minutes or until a skewer comes out clean when tested.
7) Leave to cool on a cooling rack while you make the icing.
8) To make the icing, place the tofu and cocoa into a blender or food processor.
9) Melt the chocolate by placing into a dish over a saucepan of boiling water.
10) Add the chocolate to the tofu and cocoa, and blend until smooth.
11) When icing the cakes slice the top off one of the cakes so that the other cake will sit flat on top.
12) Spread some of the icing over the flattened cake and then place the other on top and cover with the remaining icing. Decorate as desired and refrigerate before serving.

Banana Cake

A moist, sweet cake. Great for using up overripe bananas.

¾ cup plain flour
¾ cup self-raising flour
¼ tsp. bicarbonate of soda
2 tsp. mixed spice
1 tsp. ground ginger
85g vegan margarine
½ cup unrefined sugar
1 tbsp. maple syrup
¾ cup very ripe mashed banana
6 tbsp. soy or rice milk

1) Pre-heat oven to 180°C and grease and line a 25cm x 13cm loaf tin.
2) Place the flours, bicarbonate of soda, mixed spice and ginger into a medium-sized bowl and mix well.
3) In a separate large mixing bowl, cream the margarine and sugar with an electric mixer until very creamy.
4) Add the maple syrup and banana and mix well.
5) Add the dry ingredients alternately with the milk to the butter mixture. Mix gently by hand between additions and make sure you finish with the dry mixture.
6) Pour into the loaf tin and bake for 45-50 minutes or until a skewer comes out clean when tested.

Desserts

"Nature does nothing uselessly"
Aristotle

Desserts

"Thou hast given him his heart's desire."
Psalms 21:2

Shortcrust Pastry

Makes one 26cm pie crust with a top

This is a basic recipe for shortcrust pastry, good to use for sweet pies. It requires very little work to make and can be done in a food processor.

300g plain flour
115g vegan margarine
45g unrefined sugar
6 tbsp. water

1) Place flour into a mixing bowl. If you are using a food processor, place the flour into the unit and start the blade moving.
2) Cut the margarine into chunks and add to the flour. If using a processor, just keep mixing, otherwise, massage margarine into flour with fingertips until it resembles breadcrumbs.
3) Add the sugar and mix well.
4) Add the water and mix the pastry into a large ball, pressing all ingredients together.
5) Refrigerate for 1 hour.
6) When rolling pastry out for a pie, dust with flour and roll on a lightly floured surface. Wrap the rolled pastry around your rolling pin and then unroll it into your pie dish. This will prevent it breaking. Cracks and small breaks are easily repaired by pressing the pastry back together once in the pie dish, however this pastry is very flexible and you shouldn't have trouble with it breaking.
7) Continue as advised in the recipe you are using.

Shortcrust Flan Pastry

Makes one 21.5cm flan crust

This is a basic recipe for shortcrust pastry, good to use for sweet pies. It requires very little work to make and can be done in a food processor.

150g plain flour
55g vegan margarine
35g unrefined sugar
3 tbsp. water

1) Place flour into a mixing bowl. If you are using a food processor, place the flour into the unit and start the blade moving.
2) Cut the margarine into chunks and add to the flour. If using a processor, just keep mixing, otherwise, massage margarine into flour with fingertips until it resembles breadcrumbs.
3) Add the sugar and mix well.
4) Add the water and mix the pastry into a large ball, pressing all ingredients together.
5) Refrigerate for 1 hour.
6) When rolling pastry out for a pie, dust with flour and roll on a lightly floured surface. Wrap the rolled pastry around your rolling pin and then unroll it into your pie dish. This will prevent it breaking. Cracks and small breaks are easily repaired by pressing the pastry back together once in the pie dish, however this pastry is very flexible and you shouldn't have trouble with it breaking.
7) Continue as advised in the recipe you are using.

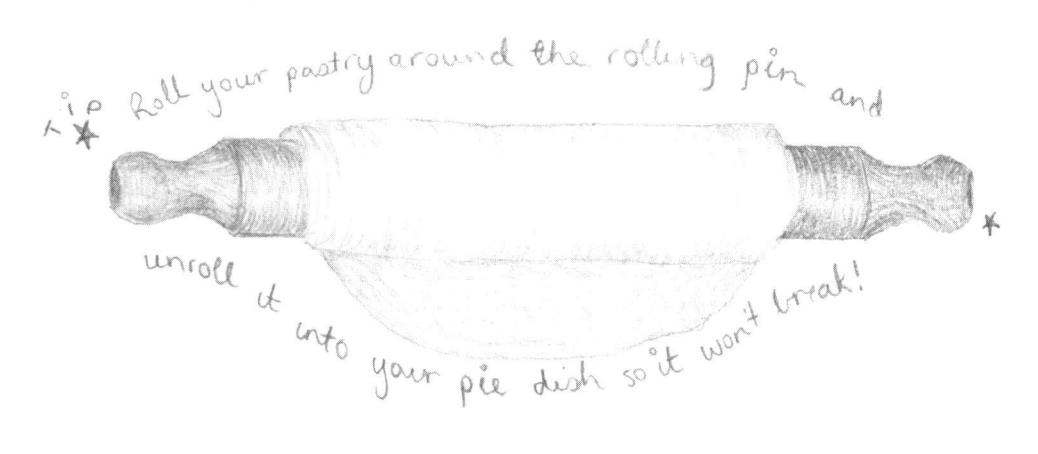

Tip: Roll your pastry around the rolling pin and unroll it into your pie dish so it won't break!

Apple Pie

This pie is flavoured with cinnamon and almonds to give it a distinctive and delicious taste. It is great served with soy custard or Cashew Whipped Cream (page 181).

creative tip: Sultanas are a good addition to this pie, or for a stonger almond flavour, try a dash of Amaretto (almond liqueur).

1 quantity of Shortcrust Pastry (p172)
950g peeled, thinly sliced cooking apples
3 tbsp. unrefined brown sugar
1½ tsp. ground cinnamon
25g slivered almonds
3 tbsp. apple juice

1) Make pastry according to directions (but only until, and including, the rolling stage).
2) Steam the apples until just tender.
3) In a large mixing bowl, combine apples with remaining ingredients, except apple juice.
4) Pre-heat the oven to 160°C.

To make the pie

1) Press two thirds of the pastry mixture into an ungreased 26cm round pie dish.
2) Spoon filling into the casing.
3) Roll out remaining pastry to form a top for the pie.
4) Lay over the top of the pie and press around the edges with a knife.
5) Poke a hole in the top (if you have managed to keep it airtight) and then brush with apple juice, which will turn the top golden as it cooks.
6) Bake for 35-40 minutes, or until golden brown.

Pumpkin Pie

This traditional American pie is, in my opinion, reminiscent of a custard tart. If you haven't tried pumpkin pie before, don't be put off by the placement of pumpkin in a dessert. It is a delicious filling! For a real treat, try serving the pie with Cashew Whipped Cream (page 181) and blueberries.

1 quantity of Shortcrust Flan Pastry (page 173)
½ tbsp. soy flour mixed with 1 tbsp. water
350g peeled pumpkin
100g silken tofu
½ cup pure maple syrup
¾ tsp. ground cinnamon
1½ tsp. mixed spice
¼ cup ground arrowroot
¼ cup rice or soy milk
¼ tsp. ground nutmeg

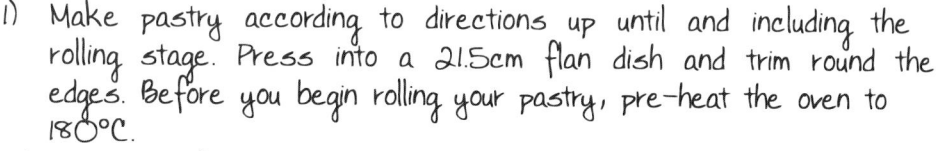

1) Make pastry according to directions up until and including the rolling stage. Press into a 21.5cm flan dish and trim round the edges. Before you begin rolling your pastry, pre-heat the oven to 180°C.
2) Brush soy flour mixture onto the base. This will form a waterproof layer and will stop the filling soaking into the pastry later on. Bake for 10 minutes, then set aside. Leave the oven on but reduce the temperature to 150°C.
3) Steam the pumpkin until tender.
4) Blend the pumpkin, tofu, maple syrup, cinnamon and mixed spice using a blender or food processor. Mix until very smooth.
5) Combine ground arrowroot and milk in a small cup, and add to pumpkin mixture. Mix well.

To make the pie

1) Pour filling into the pie shell and sprinkle the top with nutmeg.
2) Bake for 30 minutes.
3) Refrigerate for 2 hours before serving.

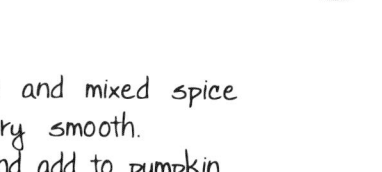

Fruit Flan

This dessert is best made 2-3 hours before to allow it to cool. You can top the flan with any fruit, although I recommend berries for both taste and presentation. You would never know that the mock custard filling is tofu!

1 quantity of Shortcrust Flan Pastry (page 173)
½ tbsp. soy flour mixed with 1 tbsp. water
350g silken tofu
5 tbsp. agave or maple syrup
2 tsp. vanilla extract
2 tbsp. ground arrowroot
fruit to decorate
¼ cup water
½ tbsp. agar agar
1 tbsp. jam (use a jam that goes with your fruit)

1) Make pastry according to directions up until and including the rolling stage. Before you begin rolling your pastry, pre-heat the oven to 180°C. Press into a 21.5cm flan dish and trim round the edges.
2) Brush soy flour mixture onto the base. This will form a waterproof layer and will stop the filling soaking into the pastry later on. Bake for 10 minutes and set aside. Leave the oven on but reduce the temperature to 150°C.
3) To make the filling, combine the tofu, syrup, vanilla extract and ground arrowroot in a blender or food processor until smooth.
4) Pour filling into the shell. Return to the oven and bake for a further 30 minutes. Chill before decorating with fruit.
5) About an hour before serving, prepare the fruit for the top of the flan (i.e. slice strawberries or kiwifruit etc.)
6) In a small saucepan, place the water and agar agar. Bring to simmer without stirring and then simmer over low heat, stirring until the agar flakes dissolve.
7) Stir in the jam.
8) Once the jam is mixed through, decorate the flan with fruit, then brush the agar agar mixture over the top of the flan, being careful not to spill onto the pastry or down the sides.
9) Refrigerate to set the jelly before serving. This should take 20-30 minutes.

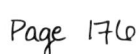

Chocolate Tart

This French-style dessert is rich and delicious. For an interesting alternative, slice fresh banana and lay on the pastry before pouring the filling over the top. Serve with Cashew Whipped Cream (see page 181) and strawberries.

1 quantity of Shortcrust Flan Pastry (page 173)
½ tbsp. soy flour mixed with 1 tbsp. water
350g silken tofu
6 tbsp. cocoa
½ cup pure maple syrup
1 vanilla pod or 1 tsp. vanilla extract
2 tbsp. ground arrowroot
100g dark vegan chocolate

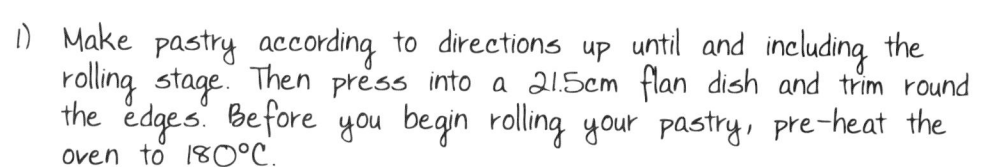

1) Make pastry according to directions up until and including the rolling stage. Then press into a 21.5cm flan dish and trim round the edges. Before you begin rolling your pastry, pre-heat the oven to 180°C.
2) Brush soy flour mixture onto the base. This will form a waterproof layer and will stop the filling soaking into the pastry later on.
3) Bake the crust for 20 minutes.
4) Once the pastry is cooked, mix all of the remaining ingredients except vegan chocolate in a blender or food processor at high speed until smooth.
5) Melt the chocolate by placing into a dish over a saucepan of boiling water.
6) Once the chocolate has melted, tip it into a small saucepan with the pureed filling ingredients.
7) Place over medium heat and stir until it boils and thickens.
8) Quickly pour the filling into the baked pie shell and refrigerate for at least 3 hours. It will set within this time, to the consistency of baked custard.

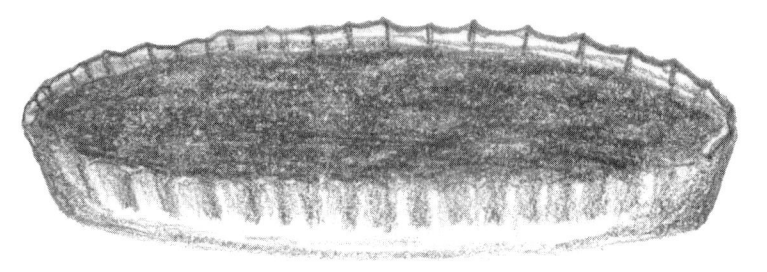

Baked Bananas with Maple and Pecan Cream

Baked bananas are delicious, especially with the flavour of fruit juices and coconut. The maple and pecan cream really finishes this dish off and is a good alternative to serving a dessert with dairy cream or ice cream

350g silken tofu
1 tsp. vanilla extract
3 tbsp. pure maple syrup
½ cup whole pecans
juice from 1 orange
juice from 1 lemon
2 tbsp. unrefined brown sugar
6 medium-sized bananas
½ tbsp. vegan margarine
5 tbsp. desiccated coconut

1) Puree the tofu, vanilla extract and maple syrup in a blender or food processor until creamy.
2) Add the pecans and blend until they are broken but not pureed (so that the cream becomes quite lumpy with the nuts).
3) Pour the cream into a serving bowl and chill.
4) Pre-heat oven to 180°C.
5) In a baking dish, combine the orange juice, lemon juice and brown sugar.
6) Peel the bananas, slice them and add to the baking dish. Mix well.
7) Break the margarine into small dabs and distribute over the banana.
8) Top with coconut and bake for 20 minutes.
9) Serve hot with the chilled cream.

Citrus Mint Burst

This is a light, summery dessert that is free from any unhealthy ingredients.

4 tbsp. tapioca
1 cup pineapple juice
1 cup orange juice
1 tbsp. agar agar flakes
1 tbsp. lemon juice
1 cup fresh chopped pineapple
1 tbsp. finely chopped mint leaves
whole mint leaves to garnish

1) Combine tapioca, pineapple juice, orange juice and agar agar in a small saucepan over medium heat.
2) Allow the mixture to boil and thicken for 10 minutes. Stir regularly during this time.
3) Remove from heat and stir in lemon juice, pineapple and mint.
4) Pour into a glass serving dish or separate dessert glasses and refrigerate until set. This will take approximately an hour.
5) Serve garnished with fresh mint leaves.

Banana and Coconut Rice Pudding

This rice pudding is a little more tropical than the traditional one. The banana and coconut give it something extra.

1 medium-sized banana
150g pudding or Arborio rice
800ml rice or soy milk
100ml pure maple syrup
½ cup desiccated coconut
1 vanilla pod or 2 tsp. vanilla extract
½ tsp. ground nutmeg

1) Pre-heat oven to 150°C.
2) Peel and chop the banana into small pieces.
3) Place banana pieces into an ungreased 20cm x 15cm baking dish and set aside.
4) Place rice, milk, maple syrup and coconut into a medium-sized saucepan.
5) Split the vanilla pod down the centre and scrape the seeds into the rice mixture.
6) Add the whole pod (or vanilla extract) and mix well.
7) Place the saucepan over medium heat and stir until the mixture starts to boil.
8) Remove from heat and pour over the banana in the baking dish. Give it a stir to make sure it is even and remove the vanilla pod skin.
9) Sprinkle the nutmeg evenly over the top of the pudding and bake for 1 hour.
10) When it is cooked, the rice should be soft and sticky, having absorbed all of the milk. Serve hot or cold.

Cashew Whipped Cream

You would never guess that this cream is made from tofu. I think it tastes a whole lot better than dairy cream and it has the added bonus of being free from animal fat.

creative tip

Try using hazlenuts, almonds or pecans instead of cashews, or, eliminate the nuts altogether and add fruit!

350g silken tofu
3 tbsp. pure maple syrup
½ cup unsalted cashews
1 tsp. vanilla extract
½ tsp. ground nutmeg

1) Place all ingredients into a food processor and mix at high speed until the mixture is thick and creamy.
2) Serve chilled with your favourite dessert.

Finale

Glossary of Ingredients

Agave syrup
A natural, liquid sweetener made from the Agave plant, which is also used to make Tequila. Although the syrup has fewer calories than sugar it is actually sweeter. Agave syrup is available in most health food shops.

Agar agar
Usually produced in flakes, it is a derivative of a Japanese red sea vegetable. It is rich in iodine and trace minerals and, when heated then cooled, produces a clear, firm jelly. It is therefore used as a replacement for gelatine, which is an animal product. Agar Agar is found in health food shops and Asian supermarkets.

Arborio rice
A short grain, white rice used in risottos and puddings for its sticky texture. Available in supermarkets.

Arrowroot
A white powdered starch extracted from rhizome plants. It is used to thicken sauces and gravies or to make puddings. You will find arrowroot in the supermarket, usually in the baking section.

Barley malt
An extract from pearl barley, this syrup is used as a sweetener. It is not as sweet as sugar and has a malt flavour. Barley malt is available in most supermarkets and health food shops.

Basmati rice
A fragrant rice from India found in supermarkets and health food shops. It costs a little more than plain, white rice but the flavour is worth it.

Blackstrap molasses
An extremely mineral rich by-product of sugarcane. It has a very strong and distinct flavour, meaning when it is included in recipes, it is not just a sugar replacement, but an ingredient put there for its specific flavour. Blackstrap molasses can be found in some supermarkets and health food shops.

Couscous
Small grains of pasta, used traditionally in Moroccan cooking. You will find it in the supermarket.

Fennel seeds
Seeds from the fennel plant which have an aniseed flavour and are delicious in Indian cooking. You can find them in large supermarkets in the spice section.

Flaxseeds
See Linseeds.

Garam masala
A spice mix used extensively in Indian cooking. It contains a ground mixture of coriander, black pepper, cumin, cardamom, turmeric, nutmeg, ginger, cloves, bay leaves, cinnamon, and chilli. You will find it in the spice section of supermarkets.

Ground arrowroot
See Arrowroot.

Lime leaves
Taken from the Kaffir lime tree, they are a very popular flavour in Thai food. You should be able to buy them from fruit shops.

Linseeds
Also known as flaxseeds, linseeds are high in omega 3 fatty acids and are great to add to your muesli or salads. You can also buy the oil extracted from the seeds (usually called flaxseed oil), but make sure that you buy it in a dark glass bottle, straight from the refrigerator. Once the oil is left at room temperature, it will go rancid. Linseeds may be found in supermarkets but the refrigerated oil is usually only found in health food shops.

Maple syrup (pure)
An extract from the leaves of the Canadian maple tree. It is a liquid sweetener, used mostly as a pancake syrup, but also to flavour baked goods. Beware of maple flavoured syrup that is full of sugar. Maple syrup is available in supermarkets.

Miso
Produced from soybeans, rice or barley and is a rich, salty condiment used to flavour many dishes. It is traditional in Japan where it is used to make soups and also to flavour most Japanese dishes. You will find miso in both the supermarket and health food shop in a variety of flavours. It comes in light, medium and dark. I have not specified which miso to use in my recipes because it is a matter of finding which taste suits you. There is no point buying a number of different packets since one packet lasts for quite some time.

Natural peanut butter
Regular brands of peanut butter usually contain excessive amounts of sugar and salt. Try buying a natural brand that contains only peanuts. You may find it in larger supermarkets, but definitely in health food shops. Some even have a machine to make the peanut butter fresh while you wait!

Pappadums
Dried lentil pancakes that swell and go crispy when fried in oil or heated in the microwave. They are a traditional Indian food eaten with curries and condiments. You will find pappadums in the supermarket.

Quinoa
Pronounced "Keen-Wa", quinoa is a grain that is slowly increasing in popularity. It contains more protein than any other grain and is also rich in minerals. Use quinoa instead of rice or add it to salads. You will find it in health food shops and in some larger supermarkets.

Rice milk
A liquid extracted from brown and white rice. Rice milk is a suitable substitute for dairy milk both as a drink and in cooking. You will find it in supermarkets and health food shops often in flavoured and plain varieties and calcium enriched. For further information, see Milk in Alternative Ingredients on page 10.

Rice mirin
A Japanese product used in cooking, which translates to rice wine. Rice mirin is available in most supermarkets and health food shops.

Rice syrup
Extracted from rice and resembles honey in consistency, but is closer to sugar in taste (although not quite as sweet). It is suitable as a spread as well as an ingredient in sweet recipes, and is usually available in both supermarkets and health food shops.

Savoury yeast flakes (nutritional yeast flakes)
Used to season soups, gravies, stews and casseroles. Savoury yeast flakes are a rich source of B vitamins, protein, amino acids, enzymes, minerals and trace elements. They are usually only found in health food shops. If you have trouble obtaining them, a vegetable stock cube is the closest alternative in taste.

Sea salt
Contains the minerals that table salt lacks. Table salt is also bleached, making it less attractive to its healthier alternative. You should be able to find sea salt in supermarkets and health food shops.

Soba noodles
Japanese noodles, made from buckwheat and wheat. They are dark brown in colour and coarser in texture than regular noodles. You may find them in the Asian cooking section of large supermarkets, otherwise, try a health food shop.

Soy milk
Liquid extracted from the soy bean. Soy milk is a suitable substitute for dairy milk both as a drink and in cooking. You will find it in supermarkets and health food shops in flavoured and plain varieties, and, calcium enriched. For further information, see Milk in Alternative Ingredients on page 10.

Soy yoghurt
Now widely available in supermarkets in both plain and flavoured varieties. It does not taste exactly like dairy yoghurt but it does behave the same way in cooking.

Tahini
A paste made entirely from sesame seeds. It is very high in calcium and usually comes in both light and dark varieties. You will find tahini in the supermarket and health food shop.

Tamari sauce
A wheat free alternative to soy sauce that is lower in salt. Tamari sauce is available in large supermarkets and health food shops.

Tamarind
The tamarind tree, originally from East Africa, now grows all over the world. It bears small fruits, which are made into pastes and liquids. The taste is citrus and very sweet. It is usually used to flavour Indian dishes. You will sometimes find tamarind in large supermarkets. If not, try the health food shop or specialty Indian/Asian supermarkets. I recommend the extract as opposed to the fruit pulp.

Textured vegetable protein (TVP)
A dry derivative of soybeans, TVP looks like large breadcrumbs and once added to liquid, takes on the appearance of minced beef and the taste of the other ingredients in your dish. Available in supermarkets and health food shops.

Tofu

The curds and whey of soy milk. Comes in a wide range of textures and tastes. You will find a variety of firm, silken and seasoned. It can be baked, boiled, broiled, grilled, or fried. It can be eaten whole, in cubes, mixed with a thousand other things to form an unlimited number of dishes. So deciding which way tofu works best for you is largely a matter of experimentation. You will find tofu in supermarkets and health food shops.

Tofu cream cheese

Cheese made from tofu. The most common brand of tofu cream cheese is Tofutti and is found in some large supermarkets and most health food shops. It has the consistency and a mildly similar taste to that of cream cheese and is perfect for use in dips and sauces.

Tortillas

A soft, flat, round bread traditionally from Mexico. Tortillas are made with wheat flour or corn and are used to wrap various fillings. They are usually found in the bread or Mexican food sections of large supermarkets.

Unrefined sugar

See sugars in Alternative Ingredients on page 13.

Vanilla pods

The original source of vanilla extract, they are long, dark and woody and contain thousands of tiny black seeds inside which taste of vanilla. They are expensive, but the best way to flavour your vanilla recipes. Available in supermarkets and health food shops.

Vegan chocolate

A dairy free chocolate, made from soy milk. Originally it was only sold in health food shops but it is gradually filtering into large supermarkets. You will find that it is quite delicious and although it may not be up to the standard of Swiss or Belgian, it is a very satisfactory substitute.

Some dark chocolates are also vegan because they contain no milk at all (dairy or soy). You will need to check the ingredients of various brands to find them.

Vegan margarine

Dairy-free margarine made from various vegetable and seed oils. There are a number on the market and the best way to decide which one is best for you is first to check the ingredients and next, to taste the ones that appeal to you. You will find various brands in large supermarkets and health food shops.

Wild rice

Contrary to what the name suggests, wild rice is actually a coarse grain. It goes well mixed with various varieties of rice, rather than eaten on its own. With this in mind, don't be surprised by the small quantities in which it is packaged. You will find it in supermarkets.

Suggested Reading List

Robbins, John "Diet for a new America" HJ Kramer Inc, California, 1987

Hartman, Thom "The Last Hours of Ancient Sunlight" Bantam Books, NZ 1999

Wigmore, Ann "Ann Wigmore's Recipes for Longer Life"

Wigmore, Ann "The Sprouting Book" Paragon Press PA, 1986

Willcox, Bradley, MD, Willcox, Craig, PhD and Suzuki Makoto, MD "The Okinawa Way" Penguin Books, Great Britain 2001

See also the websites listed in the bibliography.

Finale

Bibliography

Green, Aliza, "The Bean Bible: A Legumaniac's Guide to Lentils, Peas, and Every Bean on the Planet." Running Press Book Publishers, Philadelphia, 2000

Robbins, John "Diet for a new America" HJ Kramer Inc, California, 1987

Kulvinskas, Victoras "Survival into the 21st Century" Omangod Press, Ct USA, 1979

Milstein, Tamara "Risotto round the world" R&R Publishing, Sydney, 1996

Web Resources

Science of baking – About.com
http://busycooks.about.com/library/archive/blcakesci.htm

Vegetarian/Vegan Information
Veg Source – http://www.vegsource.com/
Australian Vegetarian Society – http://www.veg-soc.org/
International Vegetarian Union – http://www.ivu.org/index.html
Veg Family Magazine – Vegan cooking tips with Ann Gentry
http://www.vegfamily.com/ann-gentry/index.htm
Vegan's Australasian Network
http://www.vegansworldnetwork.org/van-homepage.html

Australian and New Zealand Societies

Australian Vegetarian Society

NSW
PO Box 56, Surry Hills NSW 2010
Telephone: +61 2 9698 4339   Fax: +61 2 9310 5365
Web: http://www.veg-soc.org/   Email: avs@veg-soc.org

VIC
Vegetarian Network Victoria
Ph: 0500-VEGIES (0500-834437)
Email: info@vnv.org.au

ACT
Australian Vegetarian Society (ACT)
PO Box 1786, Canberra ACT 2601
Email: contact@vegetariansociety.org.au

SA
PO Box 46, Rundle Mall, Adelaide SA 5000
Email: info@vegsa.org.au

QLD
Vegetarian / Vegan Society of Queensland
1086 Waterworks Rd, The Gap, QLD 4061
Email: vegsoc_q@powerup.com.au

Vegan Society of Australia
PO Box 85, Seaford VIC 3198
Web: http://www.veganaustralia.org
Email: info@veganaustralia.org

Natural Health Society of Australia Inc.
(not-for-profit organisation)
28 / 541 High Street, Penrith NSW 2750
Telephone: (02) 4721 5068   Fax: (02) 4731 1174
Web: http://www.naturalhealth.org.au   Email: nhs@pnc.com.au

New Zealand Vegetarian Society

Auckland
P O Box 26 6664, Epsom, Auckland
Telephone (09) 523 4686
Web: http://vegsoc.wellington.net.nz   Email: jhnsfmly@ihug.co.nz

Wellington
P O Box 27-407, Wellington
Telephone:(04) 563 6610 Fax: (04) 384 3236
Email: pam.bidwell@paradise.net.nz

Christchurch
13 Jameson Ave, Christchurch
Telephone (03) 377 4337
Email: chchveg@hotmail.com

Finale

Index

A

Aduki Beans
  cooking 18
  stir fry 121
Agar agar
  glossary 182
Agave syrup
  glossary 182
Almond Spice Crunch 30
Alternative ingredients 9
  cheese 11
  eggs 12
  honey 10
  meat 9
  milk 10
  sugars 13
  yoghurt 10
American
  corn chowder 83
  pumpkin pie 175
  style breakfast potatoes 32
  style choc chip cookies 160
Apple
  and cinnamon muffins 164
  and spice porridge 31
  pie 174
Arborio rice
  glossary 182
Arrowroot
  glossary 182
Asian
  dipping sauce 147
  mekong asparagus 61
  spring rolls 54
Asparagus
  mekong 61
Australian and New Zealand Societies 191
Avocado
  mango and avocado salad 68

B

Baked Bananas with Maple and Pecan Cream 178
Baked Goodies 153
Baking
  vegan baking tips 154

Banana
  and coconut rice pudding 180
  and walnut muffins 163
  baked bananas with maple and pecan cream 178
  cake 169
  mashed, (egg replacer) 12
Barbecue
  boston barbecue beans 120
  sauce 145
Barley
  lentil and barley shephards pie 116
  malt (glossary) 182
  wild winter warm-up 80
Basil
  tomato and basil salad 71
  tomato and basil soup 76
Basmati rice
  glossary 182
Beans
  aduki bean stir fry 121
  and carrots in tomato zest 59
  and Pulses (dishes) 103
  bean and spinach stew 111
  Boston barbecue 120
  chilli con carne 106
  general cooking 14
  hazelnutty 61
  Henna's sunflower and bean pasta 125
  lentil and bean stew 112
  minestrone soup 84
  refreshing bean boost 66
  Turkish bean soup 85
Berry Chocolate Muffins 165
Bibliography 190
Biscuits
  American style choc chip cookies 160
  chocolate coconut 155
  cinnamon 156
  lemon coconut 161
  oat and malt 157
  passion stars 159
  peanut butter 158
Blackeye Beans
  bean and spinach stew 111
Blackstrap molasses
  glossary 183
Blueberry Cake 167
Bombay Potatoes 97
Boston Barbecue Beans 120
Bread crumbs
  make your own 24

Index

Breakfast
   dishes 27
   smoothie 37
Brownies
   chocolate 162
Buckwheat and Molasses Pikelets 34
Burgers
   mushroom steaks 95
   riviera 40
   summer rice 41
Burritos 118

C

Cakes
   blueberry 167
   chocolate 168
   date loaf 166
Canellini Beans
   Boston barbecue beans 120
   minestrone soup 84
   turkish bean soup 85
Canellini beans
   cooking 18
Capsicum
   roasted capsicum and cashew pesto 151
   roasted capsicum pasta 130
Carrot
   and Beans in Tomato Zest 59
   and coriander soup 74
Cashew
   and pepper gravy 142
   roasted capsicum and cashew pesto 151
   soba noodles 134
   whipped cream 181
Casseroles
   Moroccan chickpea 114
Cheese
   alternatives 11
   tofu cream (glossary) 187
Chickpeas
   cooking 19
   homous 149
   mexican bites 45
   Moroccan chickpea casserole 114
   Moroccan vegetables with couscous 90
   vegetable dhansak 108
Chilli
   con carne 106
Chocolate
   berry chocolate muffins 165
   brownies 162
   cake 168
   coconut biscuits 155
   tart 177

Cinnamon
   apple and cinnamon muffins 164
   biscuits 156
Citrus Mint Burst 179
Coconut
   banana and coconut rice pudding 180
   chocolate coconut biscuits 155
   lemon coconut biscuits 161
Conversion Tables 7
Cookies. See Biscuits
Cooking
   dried beans and lentils 14
   tips and pointers 6
Coriander
   carrot and coriander soup 74
Corn Chowder 83
Couscous
   eggplant wraps with minted couscous 100
   glossary 183
   Moroccan chickpea casserole 114
   Moroccan vegetables with couscous 90
   roasted vegetable and couscous salad 70
Cream
   baked bananas with maple and pecan cream 178
   cashew whipped 181
Creamy
   vegetable soup 81
Creative cooking 6
Crumbed Tofu Schnitzels 47
Crystal Sweeteners
   general 13
Curry
   Bombay potatoes 97
   mixed vegetable and apricot curry 92
   pumpkin & sweet potato masala 93
   vegetable curry parcels 50

D

Dahl
   Indian dahl 104
   two lentil dahl 105
Date Loaf 166
Defining Differences 4
Desserts 171
Dill
   Dilled Spinach with Mushrooms 91
   saucey garlic potatoes with dill 89
Dips
   homous 149
   refreshing guacamole 150
   roasted capsicum and cashew pesto 151
   tomato salsa 148

E

Eggplant
- bleeding 25
- wraps with minted couscous 100

Eggs
- alternatives 12
- replacer 12

F

Fennel seeds
- glossary 183

Finale 182

Flan
- fruit 176
- shortcrust flan pastry 173

Flaxseeds
- glossary (see linseeds) 183

Fresh Tomato Sauce 144

Fried Rice
- roasted pumpkin 135
- wild 136

Fruit
- flan 176
- luxurious fruit salad 36
- slush 37

G

Garam masala
- glossary 183

Gelatine
- replacement, agar agar (glossary) 182

Gentle Lentil Stew 107

Glossary of Ingredients 182

Golden Masala 110

Gravy
- cashew and pepper gravy 142

Ground arrowroot
- glossary (see arrowroot) 183

Guacamole
- refreshing 150

H

Hazelnutty Beans 61

Henna's Sunflower and Bean Pasta 125

Herb Pasta with Sun-dried Tomatoes and Spinach 127

Homous 149

Honey
- alternatives 10

I

Indian
- dahl 104
- mixed vegetable and apricot curry 92
- moorish lentil balls 44
- two lentil dahl 105
- vegetable curry parcels 49
- vegetable dhansak 108
- vegetable pilau 137

Italian. See Pasta
- minestrone soup 84
- pizza sauce 146
- salad 64
- vegetable and bean risotto 138

J

Japanese Rice Balls 46

K

Karelien Potato Pies 56

L

Lasagne
- vegetable 128

Lemon
- and thyme roast 96
- coconut biscuits 161

Lentils
- and bean stew 112
- brown, cooking 21
- gentle lentil stew 107
- green/brown, cooking 21
- Indian dahl 104
- lentil and barley shephards pie 116
- lentil loaf 115
- moorish lentil balls 44
- potato and lentil bake 113
- red, cooking 20
- riviera burgers 40
- spaghetti bolognaise 124
- tomato and lentil soup 79
- two lentil dahl 105
- vegetable dhansak 108

Lime leaves
- glossary 183

Linseeds
- glossary 183

Liquid Sweeteners
- agave syrup (glossary) 182

Index

barley malt (glossary) 182
blackstrap molasses (glossary) 183
general 13
maple syrup (glossary) 184
rice syrup (glossary) 185

Loaf
date 166

Luxurious Fruit Salad 36

M

Malt
oat and malt biscuits 157

Mango and Avocado Salad 68

Maple syrup (pure)
glossary 184

Meat
alternatives 9

Mekong Asparagus 61

Mexican
bites 45
burritos 118
patties 42
refreshing guacamole 150
tomato salsa 148
tomato salsa salad 64
Tortilla Sandwiches 49

Middle Eastern
homous 149
vegetable soup 75

Milk
alternatives 10
rice (glossary) 185
soy (glossary) 186

Minestrone Soup 84

Mint
citrus mint burst 179
dipping sauce 147
eggplant wraps with minted couscous 100
potato, pea and mint soup 82

Miso
glossary 184

Mitchell's Red Salad 67

Mixed
seed salad 71
vegetable bake 58
vegetable curry 92

Moorish Lentil Balls 44

Moroccan
chickpea casserole 114
vegetables with couscous 90

Mostly Green Salad 69

Muesli
sweet fruity 28
toasted 29

Muffins
apple and cinnamon 164
banana and walnut 163
berry chocolate 165

Mushrooms
dilled spinach with mushrooms 91
mushroom steaks 95

N

Name Variations 8
Natural peanut butter
glossary 184

Noodles
cashew soba 134
pad thai 132
satay vegetables and soba noodles 131

Not-Sausage Rolls 48

Nuts
almond spice crunch 30
baked bananas with maple and pecan cream 178
banana and walnut muffins 163
cashew and pepper gravy 142
cashew soba noodles 134
cashew whipped cream 181
chocolate brownies 162
hazelnutty beans 61
peanut butter biscuits 158
roasted capsicum and cashew pesto 151

O

Oat
and malt biscuits 157

P

Pad Thai 132
Pancakes 35
Papadums
glossary 184

Passion Stars 159
Pasta
Henna's sunflower and bean pasta 125
herb pasta with sun-dried tomatoes and spinach 127
pesto and tomato spaghetti 126
roasted capsicum pasta 130
spaghetti bolognaise 124
vegetable lasagne 128

Pastry
   shortcrust 172
   shortcrust flan 173
Patties
   Mexican 42
   mushroom steaks 95
   spicy potato 43
Peanut
   sauce 143
Peanut Butter Biscuits 158
Pepper
   cashew and pepper gravy 142
Pesto
   and tomato spaghetti 126
   roasted capsicum and cashew pesto 151
Pie
   apple 174
   Karelien potato pies 56
   lentil and barley shephards pie 116
   pumpkin (sweet) 175
Pikelets
   buckwheat and molasses 34
Pilau
   vegetable 137
Pinto Beans
   burritos 118
   lentil and bean stew 112
   mexican patties 42
Pinto beans
   cooking 16
Pizza Sauce 146
Potato
   American-style breakfast 32
   and lentil bake 113
   Bombay potatoes 97
   Karelien potato pies 56
   pea and mint Soup 82
   rosemary and lime 59
   saucey garlic potatoes with dill 89
   spicey potato patties 43
Pudding
   banana and coconut rice pudding 180
Pumpkin
   & sweet potato fusion 60
   and sweet potato masala 93
   pie (sweet) 175
   roasted pumpkin fried rice 135
   Shanta's pumpkin soup 77

Q
Quinoa
   glossary 184

R
Red Kidney Beans
   bean and spinach stew 111
   chilli con carne 106
   refreshing bean boost 66
   vegetable and bean risotto 138
Red kidney Beans
   cooking 17
Refreshing Bean Boost 66
Refreshing Guacamole 150
Rice
   banana and coconut rice pudding 180
   basmati (glossary) 182
   cooking 22
   Japanese rice balls 46
   milk (glossary) 185
   mirin (glossary) 185
   roasted pumpkin fried rice 135
   summer rice burgers 41
   syrup (glossary) 185
   vegetable and bean risotto 138
   wild fried rice 136
   wild rice salad 65
Rice and Pasta dishes 123
Riviera Burgers 40
Roasted
   capsicum and cashew pesto 151
   capsicum pasta 130
   lemon & thyme roast 96
   pumpkin fried rice 135
   vegetable and couscous salad 70
Rosemary
   and lime potatoes 59

S
Salads 63
Salsa
   tomato 148
   tomato salsa salad 64
Satay Vegetables & Soba Noodles 131
Sauces
   asian dipping 147
   barbecue 145
   fresh tomato 144
   mint dipping 147
   peanut 143
   pizza 146
Sauces & Dips 141
Saucey Garlic Potatoes with Dill 89
Savoury
   scrolls 52
   yeast flakes (glossary) 185

Index

Sea salt
 glossary 185
Sesame
 salad 67
Shanta's
 Nifty Tofu Tip 88
 pumpkin soup 77
Shortcrust
 flan pastry 173
 pastry 172
Smoothie. See Breakfast Smoothie
Snacks, Sides & Starters 39
Soba Noodles. See Noodles
Soba noodles
 glossary 185
Soups 73
Soy
 flour (egg replacer) 12
 milk (glossary) 186
 yoghurt (glossary) 186
Spaghetti
 bolognaise 124
 pesto and tomato spaghetti 126
Spicy Potato Patties 43
Spinach
 bean and spinach stew 111
 dilled spinach with mushrooms 91
 herb pasta with sun-dried tomatoes and spinach 127
 savoury scrolls 52
Split Peas
 cooking 21
 golden masala 110
Spring Rolls 54
Stew
 bean and spinach stew 111
 gentle lentil stew 107
 lentil and bean stew 112
Stir Fry
 aduki bean 121
 cashew soba noodles 134
 pad thai 132
Sugars
 alternatives 13
Suggested Reading List 189
Summer Rice Burgers 41
Sweet
 fruity muesli 28
Sweet Potato
 pumpkin & sweet potato masala 93
 pumpkin and sweet potato fusion 60

T

Tahini 186
Tamari sauce 186
Tamarind
 glossary 186
Tart
 chocolate 177
Textured Vegetable Protein (TVP)
 not-sausage rolls 48
Textured vegetable protein (TVP)
 glossary 186
Thai
 pad thai 132
 vegetable soup 78
Thyme
 lemon and thyme roast 96
Tips
 cooking tips and pointers 6
 Shanta's nifty tofu 88
 vegan baking 154
Tofu
 and vegetable dishes 87
 cream cheese (glossary) 187
 crumbed tofu/ schnitzels 47
 glossary 187
 Shanta's nifty tofu tip 88
 silken (egg replacer) 12
 vegetables and tofu in sweet tamari marinade 94
Tomato
 and basil salad 71
 and basil soup 76
 and lentil soup 79
 carrots and beans in tomato zest 59
 fresh tomato sauce 144
 herb pasta with sun-dried tomatoes and spinach 127
 pesto and tomato spaghetti 126
 salsa 148
 salsa salad 64
Tortilla Sandwiches 49
Tortillas
 glossary 187
Turkish Bean Soup 85
Two Lentil Dahl 105

U

Unrefined sugar
 glossary 187

V

Vanilla pods
 glossary 187

Page 198

Vegan
  baking tips 154
  chocolate (glossary) 187
  definition 5
  margarinie (glossary) 188

Vegetable
  and bean risotto 138
  and tofu in sweet tamari marinade 94
  creamy vegetable soup 81
  curry parcels 49
  dhansak 108
  lasagne 128
  middle eastern vegetable soup 75
  mixed vegetable and apricot curry 92
  mixed vegetable bake 58
  Morrocan vegetables with couscous 90
  pilau 137
  roasted vegetable and couscous salad 70
  satay vegetables and soba noodles 131
  stroganoff 98
  Thai vegetable soup 78

Vegetarians
  definition 4

Vitamin B12 25

W

Walnut
  banana and walnut muffins 163

Wild
  fried rice 136
  rice (glossary) 188
  rice salad 65
  winter warm-up (soup) 80

Y

Yoghurt
  alternatives 10